YSL.COM

THE
PITCHFORK
REVIEW

Alternative uses for The Pitchfork Review

Love interest

place mat

hat

mouse pad

Pillow

weapon

a gift

coffee table centerpiece

megaphone

Demi Adejuyigbe — Andy Beta

Amy Blue — Laura Callaghan

Kris Chau — Corban Goble

David Godlis — Maria Ines Gul

Sam Lefebvre — Michaelangelo

Matos — Evan Minsker

Haley Mlotek — Dan Monick

J.R. Nelson — Camilla Perkins

Lisa Jane Persky — Marianna

Ritchey — Alex Schubert

Scott Seward — Alfred Soto

Dave Swindells — Carvell Wallace

The Pitchfork Review is a registered trademark of Advance Magazine Publishers Inc. Copyright © 2015 Condé Nast. All Rights Reserved. Printed in the U.S.A.

The Pitchfork Review No. 8, Fall 2015 (ISBN 978-0-9913992-7-7) is published four times per year by Condé Nast, which is a division of Advance Magazine Publishers Inc. *The Pitchfork Review* Principal Office: 3317 W. Fullerton Ave., Chicago, IL 60647.
Condé Nast Principal Office: One World Trade Center, New York, NY 10007.
S. I. Newhouse, Jr., Chairman Emeritus; Charles H. Townsend, Chairman; Robert A. Sauerberg, Jr., Chief Executive Officer and President; David E. Geithner, Chief Financial Officer; Jill Bright, Chief Administrative Officer.

Subscription rate in the U.S. for 4 issues is $49.99. Address all editorial, business, and production correspondence to Ryan Kennedy at ryank@pitchfork.com. Address all advertising inquiries to Matthew Frampton at matt@pitchfork.com. For permissions and reprint requests, please contact info@thepitchforkreview.com. *The Pitchfork Review* is distributed by Publishers Group West and printed by Palmer Printing Inc., 739 S. Clark St., Chicago, IL 60605. Visit us online at thepitchforkreview.com. To subscribe to Condé Nast magazines on the World Wide Web, visit www.condenastdigital.com.

COVER BY DAN MONICK STYLING: GENA TUSO AT JED ROOT MAKEUP: AMY CHANCE AT CELESTINE HAIR: SIENREE DU AT CELESTINE MODEL: MORGAN ANTUSH PROPS: RENE NAVARETTE

"'The reason for all this, of course, was *Dirty Mind*, which Jean Williams—*Billboard*'s founding R&B editor—tut-tutted over: 'The front cover has Prince standing donned in an open jacket with a handkerchief around his neck and in a pair of black briefs. Maybe it's meant to be sexy. The back cover gets better (or worse). Prince is lying down with the same 'outfit ... '" —PAGE 108

Ryan Schreiber
Editor in Chief, Pitchfork

Chris Kaskie
President

Michael Renaud
Vice President

Mark Richardson
Executive Editor

Ryan Kennedy
Director of Operations

Jessica Hopper
Editor in Chief, The Pitchfork Review

Michael Catano
Deputy Editor

Laura Snapes
Senior Editor

Will Georgantas
Matthew Montesano
Copy Editors

Molly Butterfoss
Art Director

Joy Burke
Jessica Viscius
Graphic Design

Molly Raskin
General Manager

Erik Sanchez
Christian Storm
Contributing Photo Editors

Jojo Sounthone
Design Intern

Matthew Frampton
VP, Sales

Megan Davey
VP, Finance

RJ Bentler
VP, Video Programming

Matthew Dennewitz
VP, Product

Mark Beasley
Andrew Gaerig
Neil Wargo
Developers

Ryan Dombal
Brandon Stosuy
Editorial

Charlotte Zoller
Social Media Manager

Amelia Dobmeyer
Operations

The process of writing, editing, revising, designing, and printing a magazine makes *The Review*, by its very nature, a document about musical history. This issue we look at how that history changes or gets lost by virtue of how it is recorded, and who is telling it.

In the cover story, we see how Prince worked to route *Dirty Mind* around racial barriers within the music industry. In our Q&A with Martin Sorrondeguy, he discusses the work he's done to chronicle latino punk worldwide, displacing the myth that his band, Los Crudos, was the first or only one in that scene. Critic Haley Mlotek looks at what happens when ephemera like Chuck D's boombox are put behind glass, preserved forever in institutions. Andy Beta visits Alice Coltrane's ashram and considers her legacy, one that few jazz fans allow. And—as almost every story about art and music in the eighties and nineties must—we reckon with the ghosts of a generation felled by AIDS and consider not only what could've been, but also what was born of crisis and mourning. We consider both foreverness and the never was.

This issue marks the end of our second year, and we're already hard at work on what's next. Like Luther Vandross sang, "We've come a long way and yet this is only the beginnin'."

—Jessica Hopper, Editor in Chief

fl

flipbait

*Flipbait is the section of the Review
where you feel alive again*

A Review of Every Album I Missed This Year

It's hard to listen to every album released in a year, but that doesn't mean we can't criticize them!

BY DEMI ADEJUYIGBE

SLEATER-KINNEY
NO CITIES TO LOVE

MARK RONSON
UPTOWN SPECIAL

In an early January drop, Sleater-Kinney returns with a raw powerhouse album that takes inspiration from Ramones-era punk and morphs it into something beautifully familiar, but strikingly original. Or so I've been told. I missed this album because I was stuck in a well for nine months in 2015.

Though he was born and bred in England, Ronson is known as a Hollywood hit maker in the pop community. It's no surprise he's responsible for "Uptown Funk," a song so charmingly funky that it gets even the most jaded among us dancing. If only I'd heard the rest of the album before falling into that well I was stuck in for nine months in 2015.

MORE!

BRANDON FLOWERS
THE DESIRED EFFECT

The difference between Brandon Flowers's debut and his second solo effort is the difference between day and night (or *Day and Age*, rather). Credit goes to producer Ariel Rechtshaid, who makes his career out of raising indie music to a higher standard. *The Desired Effect* elevates Flowers's writing right past any standard held by any previous Killers album. I only wish I had requested they play the final track as the firemen pulled me from the well where I was stuck for nine months in 2015.

YOUNG THUG
BARTER 6

When Young Thug hit it big in 2014, his eccentric style and oft-unintelligible lyrics drew comparisons to Dennis Rodman and Die Antwoord—*was he for real*? On *Barter 6* he eschews those comparisons and makes it clear that he is in fact realer than ever. It's a shame I had to eat this record for sustenance rather than listen to it, as I was stuck in a well for nine months of 2015.

BIG SEAN
DARK SKY PARADISE

DSP's first single, "I Don't Fuck with You," had a five-month lead time that put it at the top of the charts prior to its release. On this third album, more so than ever, Big Sean proves that his ability to put out hits is a direct result of putting in the hours. This one came out two months after I was in the well so I didn't even hear about it until, like, yesterday.

JOE SATRIANI
SHOCKWAVE SUPERNOVA

When does Joe Satriani find time to sleep? In 2015 the "Satch Boogie" solo star returned full force with *Shockwave Supernova*, a groovy instrumental album that soars between office picnic jams and the wild soundtrack of a surf competition. Some criticize Satriani for not evolving out of his niche, but the firefighters who led the rescue effort o pull me from the well and I both agree—evolution is for musicians who haven't hit their high mark, and Satriani did it so long ago that everything since has just been practice.

CHRIS BROWN & TYGA
FAN OF A FAN

It's no surprise that two of hip-hop's most unlikeable stalwarts coming together would create something unpalatable, but *Fan of a Fan* takes those very low expectations … and doubles them. Not even guest verses from Boosie Badazz and Schoolboy Q save the album in the face of its overwrought clichés and repetitive themes. I'm very glad I didn't get a chance to hear this album because I was stuck in a well for nine months of 2015.

MODEST MOUSE
STRANGERS TO OURSELVES

As Modest Mouse's first album in eight years, *Strangers to Ourselves* was almost destined to be a disappointment. But in spite of unfair expectations, Modest Mouse manages to pump out a record that camouflages itself squarely into their discography. I heard this album faintly coming from a house a few yards away from the well I was stuck in for nine months of 2015.

MUMFORD & SONS
WILDER MIND

Just as *The Desired Effect* proves that change can be a gift, Mumford & Sons' *Wilder Mind* proves that it's a gift you don't always wanna hold on to. Mumford took the folk rock that made their previous albums inescapable and turned it into the forgettable *Neon Trees* album. Good thing returning this album to the store was the very first thing I did after escaping that well, in which I was stuck for nine months.

Howard Werth & the Moonbeams

King Brilliant
Rocket Records, 1976

Released in the UK in 1975 on the ever-excellent Charisma label, and then in the USA the following year on Elton John's mostly horrible Rocket Record Company label, Howard Werth's *King Brilliant* landed in stores and then was promptly forgotten by everyone on earth. Thanks to Elton's sweet distro deal with MCA in the States, there are still plenty of lightly used copies to be found along with all the Kiki Dee and Nigel Olsson records that Sir Reg failed to sell.

Howard Werth was the lead singer in the band Audience. They teetered precariously on the third rung of British art rock, playing a lot of aromatic British shed festivals with such like-minded sod busters as Capability Brown, Family, Barclay James Harvest, and Wishbone Ash. Audience would never have the hit-making prowess of their contemporaries in 10cc or Supertramp, but they did have the sort of progressive, rural integrity that appeals to a certain breed of natural-food aficionado.

As far as records on the famous Charisma Label go, *King Brilliant* isn't as brilliant as *King Progress* by Jackson Heights (how many records are?), but it does feature two actual great songs, and sometimes that's all you need to get you through the day. Most of the album is filled with Howard's cracked nasal warble and his very British nostalgic/revisionist take on horn-filled pop rock. There are harmonicas and there is even some whistling. It's the childhood memory of a seaside show band doing tame covers of fifties American dance hits, refracted and reconstituted in adulthood through the warped lens of a seventies literate and loony libertine mind. This sound was more common than you might think.

In the midst of this trip down the garden path—as pleasant and entertaining as it is—are the seamlessly connected "Got to Unwind" and "The Embezzler." So good, and inexplicably forsaken—they are hiding in plain sight on an album that Howard himself probably doesn't even remember making. "The Embezzler" is about a longtime employee who makes out like a bandit. God only knows what "Got to Unwind" is meant to evoke. There are zombies in a zoo and jivin' "sandboys," whatever the hell they are. Both songs come across as conversational and tossed off but somehow remain epic in their emotional scope. It's a really hard trick to pull off—Gary Farr managed to do it on *Addressed to the Censors of Love* in 1973 (check out "Wailing Wall"). Howard digs deep compositionally and also manages to rein in his prog vocal tics. A no-big-deal sublimity rules the day and *King Brilliant* is all the better for it. Howard's not feeling right and his head is too light and his face is white and he's high as a kite and begging that the ugly water doesn't burst his dream balloon. We've all been there. For a brief moment in time, his dream balloon remains intact long enough for him to reach pop-prog heights of pure pleasure.

Circulation Desk

Examining American Dance Music Culture in the DJ Booth and Beyond

Somewhere right now, in a better world, there is a crowded dance floor and a kid experiencing strange new feelings for the first time. Dancers' bodies press together and apart and together again, moving across the darkness and light of a club, cornfield, empty warehouse, or sports arena. A DJ in the mood can exert the power to craft a kind of narrative in song with rises and falls in volume and tempo. The dancers hopefully respond, and maybe the kid notices as dozens of hands wave together in the air. In a sense, every dance floor is a new beginning, a universe somehow apart from civilization, even if only for a few hours, available if the crowd wants badly enough to help the DJ create that communion of unified movement and desire.

In his new history *The Underground Is Massive: How Electronic Dance Music Conquered America*, critic Michaelangelo Matos and a dozen LP crates' worth of DJs, musicians, promoters, rave kids, journalists, record label owners, and A&R reps make the argument that when it comes to sorting out the odyssey of how dance music eventually exploded across the United States, often the most important story is the party itself.

Matos traces the genre's forward-and-back trajectory toward pop ubiquity from the house-and-techno-fueled juice-bar parties of Chicago and Detroit in the early eighties to its current status as commercial (and, if you're feeling generous, cultural) juggernaut of festival meccas like Electric Daisy Carnival in Las Vegas. He chronicles rain-soaked, chemically addled rural raves and ill-timed package tours of the nineties weighed down by superstar baggage, all in an at-

> **READING LIST**
>
> *The Underground Is Massive: How Electronic Dance Music Conquered America*
> by Michaelangelo Matos
> (2015, Dey Street Books)
>
> *Legions of Boom: Filipino American Mobile DJ Crews in the San Francisco Bay Area*
> by Oliver Wang
> (2015, Duke University Press)

tempt to demonstrate how EDM has often been prey to incidental happenstance, malevolent law enforcement, and glorious hedonism.

By now it's a cliché that the very top tier of legendary DJs, from Larry Levan to DJ Harvey, have aimed higher than simply spinning the hottest records to the biggest, most jacked crowds and have taken on roles more akin to dance-floor mythologists. Like those legendary DJs, Matos is a born storyteller. In the manner of a well-curated DJ set, his book is broken up into chapters and organized around recognizable bangers—a series of legendary individual parties that cap-

tured the essence of a moment in EDM's storied history. Some are small but totally turnt local affairs like the Power Plant house music parties in Chicago in the early eighties (R.I.P. Frankie Knuckles) and the first Storm Rave on Staten Island in 1992, while others are massive events like the supremely ugly bro-ified riot and rape debacle of Woodstock '99. Even successful, scene-revitalizing events like the 2000 Detroit Electronic Music Festival seem to teeter on the brink of constant disaster. Matos digs in, investigating the myriad creative forces, including drugs, record label chicanery, and artistic ambition, that incubated and sometimes overwhelmed the spirit of these archetypal ragers.

A dizzying cast of characters filter in and out of *The Underground Is Massive*. Moby emerges as a *Twin Peaks*–sampling techno whiz kid, sells a few million records, and ends up tangled in a puppet-fueled beef with Eminem live on the MTV VMAs. David J. Prince gets involved in the scene as an enthusiastic rave zinester and becomes a national journalist and party promoter while still finding time to dance naked to Aphex Twin atop wet speakers as the 1994 Further party burns up a rainy Wisconsin campground. New York techno DJ and promoter Frankie Bones spins records at a UK bash in 1989 and brings the heat straight home, firing up a series of Storm Rave parties across the boroughs of New York City, eventually starting the label and record store Sonic Groove. The lengthy tale of French duo Daft Punk offers a key narrative that approaches dance-floor manifest destiny: flitting from their early-nineties Beach Boys–inspired rock band Darlin' to their first (helmetless!) US show to slamming out jams from their famous flashed-out pyramid at Coachella '06 all the way to eventual Grammy dominance via their pristinely luxurious album *Random Access Memories*. No spoilers, but the book ends at their Grammy after-party with EDM's most celebrated masters at work surrounded by Madonna, McCartney, Jay Z, and Beyonce—taking their rightful place among pop music's conquering icons.

Throughout the book's four hundred dense pages there are scores of other movers and shakers and genres to sort out, and Matos does a yeoman's job of not letting us get lost along the way. As a respected and incisive journalist whose work has been featured in every rag and website that cares about dance music, his bustling narrative manages to strike a balance between encyclopedic knowledge and restraint. He deftly avoids "you

A DJ in the mood can exert the power to craft a kind of narrative in song. The crews' rock-the-party-first mentality and DIY spirit sowed seeds that would flower into one of the world's most vibrant turntablist scenes.

should've been there, man" nostalgia, instead allowing his subjects' ceaseless enthusiasm for the future to mostly speak for itself. Whether that kind of future is a siren song that calls you to wave your hands in the air or not seems largely beside the point—another big party will always be on the horizon, with a flock of new kids more than down to blow it up.

Oliver Wang's more sociologically inclined new book, *Legions of Boom: Filipino American Mobile DJ Crews in the San Francisco Bay Area,* is as laser-focused as Matos's is expansive, but thankfully manages to be no less engaging or illuminating.

Wang goes deep on a scene that originally thrived on small-scale cultural and social capital, remaining almost totally ignored by mainstream media attention until long after its most notable alumni (including DMC World Champions and Invisibl Skratch Piklz DJ Qbert and Mixmaster Mike) were already filling clubs around the world.

Wang's considerable research includes an in-depth examination of immigration trends and suburban settlement patterns among Bay Area Filipinos, as well as candid interviews with DJs, promoters, and other participants. He gives a thorough analysis of the scene's focus on male homosocial bonding and includes a welcome and much-needed consideration of why women were so often left out of the scene's crews. Rather than being weighed down by an overly academic tone, Wang

makes it easy to understand why he finds the scene worth celebrating: *Legions of Boom* makes the case that the crews' rock-the-party-first mentality and DIY spirit—buying or renting their own helicopter lights and smoke machines and honing their blending chops to shake the rafters of teen centers, church fairs, and neighborhood backyard parties—sowed seeds that would flower into one of the world's most vibrant turntablist scenes. He then goes on to show how the turn away from dance-floor synchronicity to a focus on technical virtuosity brought the original scene largely to a close.

While these books obviously rely on wildly different playlists, Wang and Matos each spin a tale that finds the same optimistic tempo. Even when Matos casts a jaundiced eye on contemporary EDM (he can't help but bellyache that Swedish House Mafia "could give Bryan Adams insulin shock"), much of the genre's forward momentum seems to have him in thrall. Instead of endlessly mourning a microscene largely forgotten by history, Wang celebrates the trails it blazed and the new generations of party throwers and club kids—including the children of those Filipino Bay Area crews' original leading lights—and where those trails might eventually take them. Both writers seem to argue that as long as each quasi-legal party, DJ set, and local dance scene still to be born represents a possible new beginning, the future will remain as wide open and deep in the groove as ever. ✐

Finding Heroes in Memphis Cemeteries

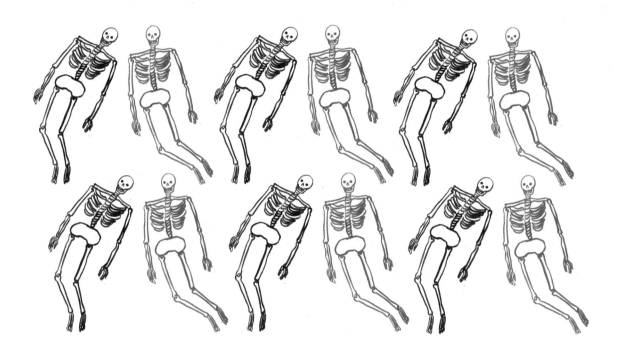

Everyone knows where Elvis is buried, but the Birthplace of Rock 'n' Roll is also the final resting place of several other icons responsible for some of the best music ever. We give you the points of latitude and longitude you need to find them.

BY EVAN MINSKER

Memphis is haunted. It's a rock 'n' soul Valhalla that offers constant reminders of bygone eras and dead icons, for a price. Tour Sun Studio and the guide will point out the exact spots where Sam Phillips, Elvis Presley, Johnny Cash, and Carl Perkins all stood. The Stax Museum is lined with memorabilia once owned by leading lights of Memphis soul. People smile as they're photographed in front of the Lorraine Motel—now the National Civil Rights Museum—as they pose at the site of Dr. Martin Luther King Jr.'s murder.

One of its biggest tourist attractions is a grave: Elvis Presley is buried in his own yard (35.04527, -90.02285), not far from where he expired. Graceland is a monument to excess, and if you want to get past the gate you'll have to fork over a sizable pile of money. It's not a private place to pay your respects by any means—you're probably going to be shoulder to shoulder with a legion of international admirers wrangling smartphones and listening to an audio tour narrated by John Stamos. For a man whose life was hardly private, this all seems perfectly fitting.

The King is just one of many musical icons buried in the city; Jay Reatard (born Jimmy Lee Lindsey Jr.) is another. His headstone in Memorial Park Cemetery (35.108637, -89.874165) features the words MEMPHIS PUNK ROCKER and a relief of two Flying V guitars crossed like swords. It's a spot right across from the Crystal Shrine Grotto—a trippy man-made cave full of biblical scenes rendered in rock quartz crystal and semiprecious stones that's worth a visit. However, Reatard's other neighbors might be just as unique: he's buried directly to the left of Isaac Hayes, and Johnny Cash's bassist, Marshall Grant, is close by to his right.

Memphis is a living, vibrant city—it's one of the country's great hubs of barbecue, beer, and bold, worthwhile music, and it's home to one of the best record stores in the country (Goner, duh). It's a city whose culture has been shaped by countless musicians, both famous and obscure, and the next time you're in town, take a minute to pay your respects.

> "Memphis is a rock 'n' soul Valhalla that offers constant reminders of bygone eras and dead icons, for a price."

Chris Bell
Jan. 12, 1951–Dec. 27, 1978
Memphis Funeral Home & Memorial Gardens
35.227222, -89.786667

Christopher Branford Bell grew up in a wealthy family in the Memphis suburb of Germantown. Like a lot of kids in the late sixties, he played in bands and worshipped the Beatles. He learned how to engineer at Ardent Studios, where he reunited with his old friend Alex Chilton and hatched a plan to start what would become Big Star. The band's debut, *#1 Record,* was a commercial flop, and Bell took it hard. Distraught and frequently using drugs, he quit the group and attempted suicide before becoming a born-again Christian. Though he recorded some of his best songs after Big Star, his attempts to get a solo record deal failed. He died in a Memphis car crash in 1978 at the age of twenty-seven. A collection of his solo songs, *I Am the Cosmos*, was released posthumously in 1992.

ESSENTIAL WORKS "I Am the Cosmos," "You and Your Sister," *#1 Record* (especially "Try Again")

James Carr
Aug. 4, 1942–Jan. 7, 2001
Lakeview Memorial Gardens
35.042778, -90.123056

Though he never became a star, James Carr was one of the most talented soul singers in the world. The Memphis-raised Mississippean's 1966 recording of "The Dark End of the Street" is considered to be definitive. It stands as his most famous work; the song is referenced on his headstone. He was never a showman like Otis Redding or James Brown, but his voice was expressive and big. His career was stifled by his struggles with mental illness, yet his recordings on Goldwax are among the best soul sides ever. He returned to music in the nineties, releasing a pair of albums and touring. He died from lung cancer in 2001.

ESSENTIAL WORKS "The Dark End of the Street," "These Ain't Raindrops," "You've Got My Mind Messed Up"

Rufus Thomas
Mar. 26, 1917–Dec. 15, 2001
New Park Cemetery
35.02468, -90.0673

Rufus Thomas was born a sharecropper's son in Casey, Mississippi. A consummate entertainer and vaudevillian, he was best known for his singles on Stax, most of which were soul tunes nominally about animals ("Walking the Dog," "Do the Funky Chicken," "Can Your Monkey Do the Dog"). He also gave Sun Records its first-ever hit with "Bear Cat." He was a wide-eyed, goofy, dancing presence on the stage and he billed himself appropriately as "the World's Oldest Teenager." His brief appearance in Jim Jarmusch's *Mystery Train* is one of the film's best moments.

ESSENTIAL WORKS "Memphis Train," "Walking the Dog," "Tiger Man"

Bobby "Blue" Bland
Jan. 27, 1930–Jun. 23, 2013
Memorial Park Cemetery
35.105, -89.873611

Bland was born in Millington, north of Memphis, and grew up singing spirituals. He came to the blues through his love of T-Bone Walker and became a pioneer by combining that sound with slick big-band arrangements. He was wildly influential—the Grateful Dead, Van Morrison, and the Band all covered his work. As of publication, Bland's grave is unmarked. A Memorial Park Cemetery employee said that his family were still getting their financial affairs in order and that he'll have a proper headstone soon. For the time being, the only way to find Bland's grave is to ask one of the cemetery's employees, who will take you there on a golf cart.

ESSENTIAL WORKS "It's My Life Baby," "Turn On Your Love Light," "Ain't No Love in the Heart of the City"

Sam Phillips
Jan. 5, 1923–Jul. 30, 2003
Memorial Park Cemetery
35.107311, -89.873525

As the founder of Sun Studio, Sam Phillips is the man responsible for the earliest recordings of Howlin' Wolf, Elvis Presley, Rufus Thomas, Carl Perkins, Jerry Lee Lewis, B.B. King, Johnny Cash, Roy Orbison, and legions of others. He started the Memphis Recording Service as an attempt to record the blues, but he also worked the console for weddings, commercials, and funerals. Phillips was even behind the console for the first known recording of distorted guitar. He's buried in one of the largest mausoleums in the South, so it's easiest to locate his grave (and that of Donald "Duck" Dunn, who's also buried here) with the assistance of a cemetery employee. Ask for Butch Valentine.

ESSENTIAL WORKS Elvis Presley's *The Sun Sessions*, any Sun Records box set

Willie Mitchell
Mar. 1, 1928–Jan. 5, 2010
West Tennessee State Veterans Cemetery
35.038333, -89.754722

Willie Mitchell was one of the most important and well-connected figures in Memphis music history. He worked with Sam Phillips and started jazz bands that inspired future Stax session players. His own instrumental work proved his mastery over the Memphis soul sound, but when he linked up with Al Green, the two men made classic records and ushered in a new era of Memphis music history. Mitchell became the chief operating officer of Hi Records in 1970 and led that label through its most successful era. He was drafted by the army in 1950 and did a short stint in a service band, so you'll find him buried in the West Tennessee State Veterans Cemetery. The graves are organized in a grid—Mitchell is at Q10251.

ESSENTIAL WORKS "Soul Serenade," "Willie's Mood," Al Green's *I'm Still in Love with You*, Ann Peebles's "I Can't Stand the Rain"

Estelle S. Axton
Sept. 11, 1918–Feb. 24, 2004
Charles E. Axton
Feb. 17, 1941–Jan. 1974
Forest Hill Cemetery East
35.192297, -89.833838

Estelle Axton was the cofounder of Stax Records. Her son, Charles "Packy" Axton, was the tenor sax player and leader of Stax's mainstays the Mar-Keys. It wasn't Estelle's intention to start a soul label—she and her brother Jim Stewart were interested in releasing music from all sorts of genres—but thanks to Rufus and Carla Thomas, soul music was their first success. The Axtons are buried next to each other at Forest Hill Cemetery East. Estelle also has a memorial bench featuring the Stax logo beneath a tree nearby.

ESSENTIAL WORKS Any Stax box set, the Mar-Keys' "Last Night"

Donald "Duck" Dunn
Nov. 24, 1941–May 13, 2012
Memorial Park Cemetery
35.107311, -89.873525

Al Jackson Jr.
Nov. 27, 1935–Oct. 1, 1975
New Park Cemetery
35.02684, -90.06843

Booker T. and the MGs were the Stax Records house band, but unlike Motown's Funk Brothers, they weren't forced to exist in the shadows: they toured on their own and had instrumental hits. Jackson provided the percussive backbone for the early Stax catalog. Dunn, who also famously played in the Blues Brothers Band, provided the MGs' sturdy, looping bass lines. Jackson's headstone at New Park Cemetery features a drum kit. Dunn is buried in the same Memorial Park mausoleum as Sam Phillips.

ESSENTIAL WORKS "Green Onions," "Tic-Tac-Toe," "Hip Hug-Her"

Ronnie Caldwell
Dec. 27, 1948–
Dec. 10, 1967
Memorial Park Cemetery
35.1125, -89.871944

Carl Lee Cunningham
1948–Dec. 10, 1967
New Park Cemetery
35.02784, -90.06862

Jimmie King Jr.
June 8, 1949–
Dec. 10, 1967
New Park Cemetery
35.02784, -90.06862

Phalon Jones
1948–Dec. 10, 1967
New Park Cemetery
35.02667, -90.06689

The Bar-Kays were another Stax staple. In 1967, they released the single "Soul Finger" and were chosen to be Otis Redding's backing band. The four members listed above were all killed in the plane crash that killed Redding. King, Cunningham, and their seventeen-year-old valet Matthew Kelly are buried next to each other in New Park Cemetery. Jones is nearby, while Caldwell's grave is across town at Memorial Park.

ESSENTIAL WORKS "Soul Finger," "Pearl High"

For a Google Map of all of these locations, head to p4k.co/S33vS. All GPS coordinates and locations are approximate. If you need help locating someone, ask for assistance during the cemetery's office hours. Please be respectful and bring flowers.

A Little Bird Told Me

The History of Musical Notation

Have you ever thought about how weird it is—philosophically, I mean—to write down or record music? Music is a temporal art; it's made of sound, and sound cannot be frozen in time for its details to be analyzed. With a painting, you can point and say, "Look at this particular shade of green," or "See how Judith is sawing off the head of Holofernes." With a book or a poem, you can debate subtext, tone, or metaphor, but at least there are the inarguable details of the words on the page, a unified starting point from which we can all begin. Music, on the other hand, dissipates in the moment of its becoming. It's like smell—ephemeral, lingering in the imagination rather than in actual space.

If you try to imagine recording or writing down a smell, you can begin to see the conceptual problem faced by those who, roughly a thousand years ago, started trying to notate music. Up to that point, music was a purely orally transmitted art (for the most part—the Greeks had a rudimentary system of notation, but we can't decipher it). You could only learn a song from someone who already knew it; there was no way to pass a melody on except by singing it. But really, who cares? Just as we do not find it odd that smells cannot be written down, neither did the ancients find the lack of musical notation frustrating.

This state of affairs only appears troubling if you look at it within the context of the Roman Catholic church, which back then was simply called the Church. If there's one thing you know about Catholicism, it's probably that Catholicism involves priests. But what you might not have known is that in olden times, these priests were primarily *singers*. They didn't really think of themselves that way—as musical performers (sinful! egotistical!)—but the fact remains that the Catholic liturgy consisted of a lengthy, highly ritualized series of biblical texts, the sung performance of which is called "chant" or "plainchant."

What were the melodies, then, that these texts were to be chanted to, day in and day out, in reverence and worship of our Lord? In order to chant all these texts together every day, clergy needed to know the same melodies, otherwise it would've just been a weird cacophony, unpleasing to the ear of God. So priests all over Europe handed down the chant melodies, generation after generation, by teaching them, orally, to each successive new wave of young acolytes. And the crucial thing to remember is that we aren't talking about ten or twelve or forty chant melodies, we're talking about THOUSANDS of them, because they sang a different melody for each liturgical text depending on the date of the calendar year. And these thousands of chant melodies not only had to be taught orally, they had to be REMEMBERED, without the aid of a musical score or recording of any kind.

The transmission of the church liturgy is one of the classic bits of anecdotal evidence medievalists point to in order to demonstrate the almost supernatural superiority of ancient memory capacities when compared to our shitty modern ones. Back then, not only was everyone illiterate, but paper was incredibly expensive. You couldn't just write down a tidal chart or what date you should plant which crop on or what percentage of tax ought to be levied upon which small landowner or whatever else; you had to remember that stuff, using just your brain. They did fantastically complex math in their heads and then KEPT it there. They remembered stuff that now we need day planners and iCal reminders and human secretaries to enable us to even vaguely keep track of. You know a farmer's almanac? That huge book that tells you all the data about seasons and soil and frosts, and about the dates all these things have happened on for the past ten years? A medieval farmer—even a stupid one!—had all that stuff in his head, like no big deal.

So, to become a priest, you went to the closest nearby priest-training facility and spent basically ten years memorizing thousands of Latin chants. Then you were a priest, and you spent the rest of your life singing those chants every day. Obviously, this practice accrued a bit of the telephone-game effect as the centuries wore on—chants unavoidably evolved and changed as they were passed from priest to priest. But, so long as all the priests in a given parish or region were singing the same melodies, it didn't seem to matter much.

In the year 768, along comes Charlemagne, and he's like, *Let's make this shit a Roman Empire again, like for real!* The Roman Empire had collapsed three hundred years earlier; Charlemagne had big dreams. And one of his major undertakings, in unifying the Roman Empire, was his attempt to minimize regional cultural differences across the land. If everyone speaks the same language and practices the same cultural traditions, in Germany and France and Italy, then surely everyone will feel united as one people, which is good for an emperor. Thus, standardizing the liturgy became enormously important—the medievals basically did church all day every day; it was a crucial feature of life. If that could be standardized, then maybe there would be no more revolts or civil wars.

Now you are beginning to see the problem that would make musical notation suddenly seem like an important idea to develop. Because if you are the Holy Roman Emperor and you want every single one of your subjects to hear the same exact melodies every day in church, from Flanders to Rome, how do you accomplish that goal? You can't just make your scribes draw up a million copies of the same chants and send them out to everyone, because musical notation doesn't exist. Instead, you have to send out human priests, who spend lifetimes crawling all over the land, laboriously teaching all these thousands of chants to every small-town priest and set of rogue monks in Christendom—guys who, up to this point, had been just kind of doing the chants of their particular region. Charlemagne wants all those guys to sing the same melodies. This is obviously an impossible task.

Adding to its impossibility is the unfortunate fact that people don't like being told that they're doing it wrong, especially when it comes to worshipping God. So Charlemagne also created some pretty epic propaganda that claimed that ages ago God sent Pope Gregory the Great the correct chant melodies in the form of a bird who flew down from heaven, placed his beak in Gregory's ear, and whispered the melodies to him. A very fun fact is that this legend is where the phrase "a little birdie told me" comes from.

So all these priests go a–horseback riding through Europe for decades and decades, arriving in some tiny village and being like, "Remember that old pope, Gregory, from hundreds of years ago? Well, it turns out a bird told him what to do in church. Anyway, put on your thinking caps because I'm going to live here for ten years and force you to memorize three thousand new melodies for these songs you've been singing your whole life."

It was only due to this suddenly pressing need for mass standardization that people started trying to figure out a way to write music down. What a bizarre idea! How would you even approach such a task? If an emperor told you to find a way to write down smells, how would you do it? I honestly don't know.

The earliest examples of musical notation are called "neumes," and they are little doodly marks borrowed from old-school rhetorical markings used to indicate vocal inflection when reading scriptures aloud. While learning a chant, maybe you'd take the piece of parchment the Latin text was written on and make a little upward squiggle to remind you that on that word you should send your voice upward. How far upward—from which note to which note—was not indicated in these markings, though, and neither was any rhythmic information (how long to hold a note relative to other notes, etc.), so neumes were merely a mnemonic device; they helped you "remember" a song you already knew. They could not be used to transmit an unknown song to a new person.

If there's one thing you know about Catholicism, it's probably that Catholicism involves priests. In olden times, these priests were primarily singers.

In the early eleventh century, real notation finally starts emerging with the invention of the musical staff, which is credited to a monk named Guido (ca. 992–1033). A staff allows notes to be standardized relative to one another, sort of, so long as we can all agree on what the intervals between staff lines are. Once you have staff lines, the rest follows more or less intuitively, although it still took three hundred more years or so before they figured out how to notate rhythms precisely.

Notation has major implications for composition itself—when music has to be held in the head, it can become only so complex before it becomes impossible. The idea of a symphony—music without any words at all, with extraordinarily long and complicated thematic development and harmonic movement among hundreds of instruments—would be unthinkable without the ability to write down all the different parts and keep track of them over the grand scale of such a work.

All of this is very interesting, but the philosophical implications of notation are even more compelling. What happens to music once it can be written down? It is turned into a THING that can be held in the hands, pointed at, and, tragically, bought and sold. The commodification of music begins here, really, in the eleventh century. The history of notation also raises immense conceptual problems. What even *is* "music"? For the Greeks, it was a manifestation of an astronomical fact—guys like Pythagoras believed that as the planets and stars whirled around in the cosmos, these heavenly bodies vibrated at different speeds, the sounds of those vibrations combining to make one shimmering, invisible chord—the "music of the spheres." This celestial harmony is unhearable by human ears, and yet we too vibrate with our own frequencies, which combine with those of animals, plants, and other people to make the music of Earth. (Those of you familiar with Sun Ra will perceive that he was reading about Pythagoras.) When we make audible music—with our voices, or with lutes or whatever—we are attempting to access this divine vibration, this sound of perfection, that our imperfect human ears can only dream of. For the Greeks, music was not entertainment but something much more profound—they thought it could actually affect human bodies and minds, that it could reshape characters and desires, that it could heal or cause sickness and injury.

For the medieval European priests, music was a way of talking to God. Surely when attempting to communicate with the divine, we should not just use our regular voices, our regular language! We should not speak to God with the same voice we use to argue with the tax man or yell at our recalcitrant children. Music—chanting—was a type of heightened speech, a special language meant only for God's ears. In fact, in orthodox Islam, for example, music is forbidden, but the imams conduct religious rites in what sounds very much like medieval chanting. They don't think of this as "music"—it's not music in the way that Katy Perry or Beethoven is music, it's not of the material world—and indeed they would be offended if you made such a comparison.

Writing music down troubles some of these ideas. It helps music become a material possession, and it also helps music become an "Art," with a capital A. Where priests a thousand years ago thought of themselves as vessels for the glory of God and not as "composers" or "performers," musical notation slowly turns music into something to be slaved over, with quill and ink, in pursuit of a "masterpiece." Does this artistic endeavor glorify God or the sinful self? The early church was worried about this question. The increasing compositional complexity made possible by notation was disturbing, for example, because it began to obscure the holy words of the texts the music was meant to convey. What *is* religious practice, anyway? What should it be about? The beauty of the music or the meaning of the words? The glory of the human voice/mind, or the awesomeness of God's power? Can these things be separated? Music continues to evade us. ✐

UK Club Scene:
The Dawn Of Rave, 1986-1990

I was lucky. I'd been taking photographs around London clubs since the mid-80s, before the potent cocktail of Acid House, Balearic Beats, and drugs made the scene crazy—long before small underground parties grew into huge outdoor raves. I was already taking club photos for *i-D* when I became Nightlife Editor for London's *Time Out* magazine in 1986, so I knew many club promoters and DJs. They knew that I was far more inclined to spread the good news rather than bust the scene wide open with a drug scandal story, so I was invited into events that other media people either didn't know about or couldn't get into. I'd witnessed ecstasy-fuelled euphoria and hysterical behaviour a couple of years before at Leigh Bowery's Taboo nights, but Paul Oakenfold's prophetically-named club night, Future, had a different kind of intensity—one that felt strangely purposeful.

What made this scene feel different was that it wasn't just seasoned clubbers and 'Soho Bohos.' At underground clubs like Shoom, Spectrum, Trip, and RIP there was a whole new crowd who dressed down to go out. Many wore baggy tops that they could sweat in along with dungarees and Converse or hi-top trainers; club door pickers who might previously have turned them away welcomed them with open arms. For a few madcap years there were all kinds of illicit adventures to be had experiencing the music in warehouses, clubs, and open fields. Social barriers seemed to dissolve as people from all walks of life partied together, which is saying a great deal in class-conscious Britain.

It was at Oakenfold's Future as well as at Danny and Jenni Rampling's necessarily-secretive Saturday nighter, Shoom, that I first experienced this sense of community, and it gave me the extra impetus to try to capture these moments on film. By the spring of 1988 that it was inevitable that this scene was going to grow rapidly; maybe I let the collective buzz sway my judgment, as I remember thinking that similar scenes could develop across America, Europe and Japan by 1990...Well, it didn't work out quite like that, but even so, what happened around the UK during those summers of love was extraordinary.

—DAVE SWINDELLS

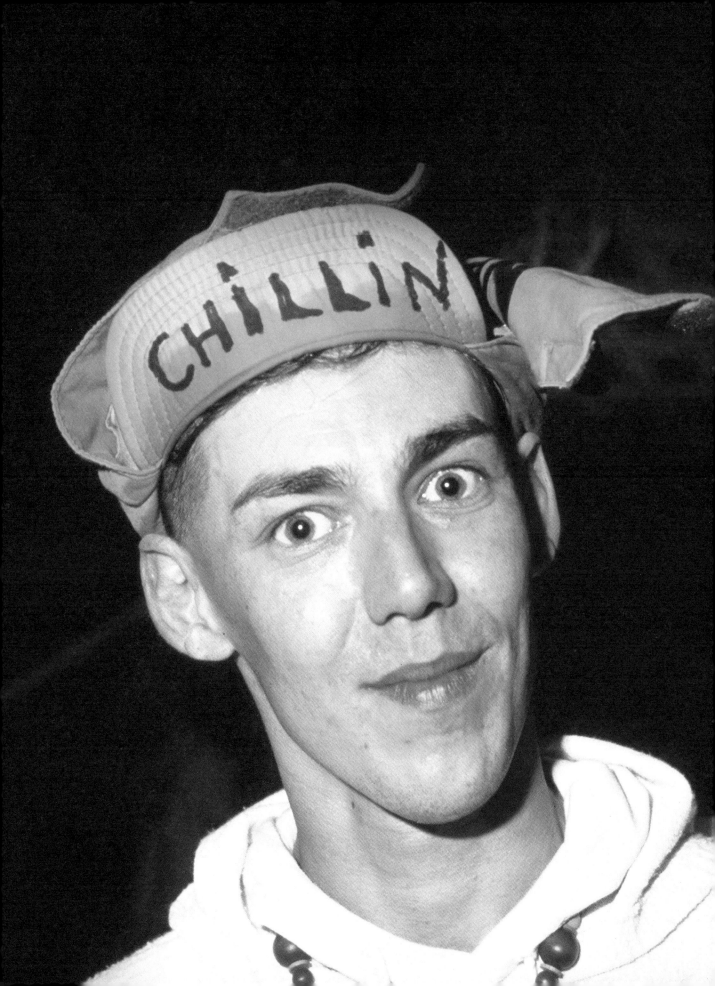

GARY HAISMAN IN THE DRY ICE AT LOVE, THE WAG, LONDON. MAY 1988.
LEFT SASHA SOUTER AT SHOOM, THE FITNESS CENTRE, SOUTHWARK, LONDON. MAY 1988.
PREVIOUS PAGE ONE OF THE SELF-STYLED 'MATLOCK MENTAL POSSE' AT A SMALL RAVE
NEAR WINCHCOMBE IN GLOUCESTERSHIRE. AUGUST 1990.

SHOOM AT THE FITNESS CENTRE, SOUTHWARK, LONDON. APRIL 1988.
RIGHT 'REACHIN,' AS THE SONG BY PHASE II SAID. THE SPECTRUM AND TIME OUT PARTY IN JUBILEE GARDENS, LONDON. JUNE 1988.
FOLLOWING PAGE A STREET PARTY IN TOTTENHAM COURT ROAD AS CLUBBERS LEFT TRIP AT THE ASTORIA, LONDON. JULY 1988.

SHOOK AT SAMURAI STUDIOS, LONDON. JULY 1988.
RIGHT DANCERS AT TRIP SEEN FROM THE BALCONY OF THE ASTORIA, LONDON. JULY 1988.
FOLLOWING PAGE WAITING IN LINE TO GET INTO TRIP AT THE ASTORIA, JUNE 1988.

DUNGAREES AND BIG SMILES AT THE SPECTRUM AND TIME OUT PARTY IN JUBILEE GARDENS, LONDON. JUNE 1988.
LEFT YOU SPIN ME RIGHT ROUND: THE GYROSCOPE AT THE FASCINATIONS AT THE DOWNHAM TAVERN IN KENT, AUGUST 1988.
FOLLOWING PAGE LET FREEDOM REIGN: TRIBAL DANCE IN GLOUCESTERSHIRE. AUGUST 1990.

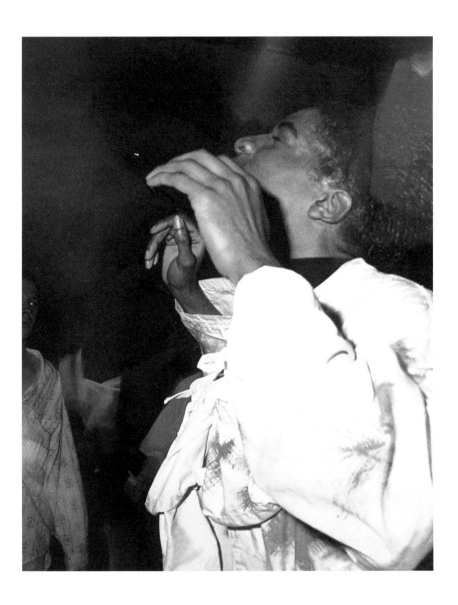

THE SPECTRUM AND TIME OUT PARTY IN JUBILEE GARDENS, LONDON. JUNE 1988.
RIGHT WATCHING THE SUNRISE AT THE BOY'S OWN PARTY NEAR EAST GRINSTEAD IN SURREY. AUGUST 1989.
PREVIOUS PAGE MICKY STACEY AND BARRY MOONCULT PULLED THE UDDER ONE INSIDE THE MAD COW
COSTUME AT THE BOY'S OWN PARTY NEAR EAST GRINSTEAD IN SURREY. AUGUST 1989.

Cosmic Neurotic

The Heady Perfectionism of Tame Impala's Kevin Parker

BY CORBAN GOBLE

I'm making my way through the backstage catacombs of Manhattan's Beacon Theatre, a stately concert hall that often hosts classic rockers like the Allman Brothers when they want to charge more than $100 for nosebleed seats. While climbing up endless Escher–style stairs, I get lost and find myself staring blankly at a bunch of the venue's grizzled employees cradling out–of–date computers.

I tell them I'm here to interview Tame Impala; they have never heard of the psychedelic rock band, but one stout lifer offers an anecdote about that time he had to fetch Eric Clapton an emergency sandwich.

Eventually, I find frontman Kevin Parker, swaddled up and nursing a hangover in a space that looks like a tastefully carpeted broom closet. Though he's surrounded by the ghosts of rock 'n' roll legend, he seems somewhat weightless and without expectation; he's most concerned about getting the night's lights right. It's late last year, and he talks about the solitary mind-set that he's trying to inhabit while creating Tame Impala's third album, *Currents*. The meeting is brief and somewhat shapeless, though one thing seems clear: the guy is very much in his own head. After a while, he picks up a call from his girlfriend, and I leave.

About six months later, I meet Parker again on the other side of America, in the California desert. He's getting ready to play Coachella with the rest of his band, though, offstage, Tame Impala is essentially a solo project. "For us, it's a big joke that we're playing these big shows," Parker says, alluding to the somewhat seat-of-the-pants approach the quintet takes on tour. "It's completely absurd because we're just us; I'm just fuckin' Kevin. We're just these fuckin' idiots onstage."

"But recording is different," he clarifies. "Because, for me, recording music couldn't be further from a joke." At this point, he has just wrapped *Currents*, an album that he recorded, produced, and mixed himself while holed up in a beachside shack in his hometown of Perth, Australia. He's still reeling from the obsessive undertaking days after sending in the final cuts. Sitting across from me in a hotel bar shopped up to look like something out of a Rat Pack movie, he doesn't look particularly well rested, or well nourished, or well anything.

"I didn't realize it would add a completely extra dimension of absolute nervous breakdowns," Parker says, talking about the new album's one-man recording process. "I was just sitting in my studio going, 'Fuck. How am I going to do this?'"

Though many artists Do It Themselves, the fact that Parker's end product sounds as deep and textured as it does is unusual. In some ways, it barely seems possible. What start as simple recordings in his studio—and sometimes even voicemails to himself—become fully rendered songs that encompass both tie-dyed headiness and an ambiguous, self-scouring ache. During the making of an album, the twenty-nine-year-old generally likes to rise around midday and then work, slowly and methodically, late into the night while drinking and smoking. He says that having a home studio means he doesn't have to drive home intoxicated; he's not a lush, but he doesn't mind taking the edge off.

Currents takes Tame Impala's core formula—old-school headphone psych with enough modern rhythmic oomph to thrill young women in bell-bottoms, graybearded Deadheads, and tucked-in business dudes—and molds it into a hybrid of classic rock, classic soul, and yacht-ready groove worthy of The Very Best of 10cc. While listening to it, the words "tie-dye hot air balloon" often find their way to the front of my skull.

The album marks the first time Parker didn't employ an outsider to help translate his trippy musings. (Both previous Tame Impala albums, 2010's *Innerspeaker* and 2012's *Lonerism*, were mixed by Dave Fridmann—the studio guru who has steered MGMT and the Flaming Lips toward many of their best moments.) Parker tells me how, while listening to his own mixes, he couldn't help fixating on imperfections. "Is the drumming in time?" he would ask himself. "Does every note of this vocal fit the song's underlying tone?"

Though Parker is on his own crusade to stretch listeners' minds, he can at times seem so deep into the music that he can't enjoy it. This obsessiveness extends all the way down to album artwork—he tells me he once sank thirty grand into a cover concept he never ended up using. While making *Currents*, Parker would try to quell his neuroses with four words of advice Fridmann often used to give him: "It doesn't fucking matter."

Despite the positive reception to *Currents'* advance tracks—which have already been collectively streamed nearly fifteen million times on Spotify—Parker himself isn't buying in to the attention, anticipation, acclaim, and money he has received in recent years. He knows these accolades mean little when he's trying to stretch his vision in a new, starker dimension.

"I still think this album is completely unlistenable," he says.

Currents maintains a different mood than the echoing moonage daydreams that made up Tame Impala's first two LPs. While Parker made his name off of recordings that you could float in and out of—such was the beauty of their surfaces—this one invites a closer listen. On the whole, it's a more heartfelt exercise, incorporating both the measure of Parker's inward-looking examinations and the pains they may have caused him.

On the album's emotional core, "Eventually," big drums drop out and shimmering synth washes put a spotlight on Parker as he sings: "I know that I'll be happier, and I know you will too—eventually." I suggest that this is his breakup record—after all, since his last album, he parted ways with French singer-songwriter Melody Prochet—but he shoots the idea down. Kind of.

"I wouldn't say it's a breakup record in the literal sense," he half dodges, before getting a little cosmic. "It's more about this idea that you're being pulled into another place that's not better or worse. It's just different. And you can't control it. There are these currents within you." Perched in a chintzy bar while a sixty-year-old man in a tuxedo vest shakes two margaritas nearby, Parker is hesitant to clarify who or what his songs are about, exactly.

But he's more than willing to elaborate on the notion of transition, of breaking up with old ideas, of how being inside the music industry has given him a new perspective on how strange and fucked up that world can be. "Your morals on things change," he explains. "When you start out you have this very black-and-white idea that people who are playing down-to-earth music are the ones that are keeping it real, and the ones making music for the masses—those 'commercial pop sellouts'—are fake, so you pick a side. But the longer you're in it, the more disappointed you get meeting people you had these high expectations of, and you realize it's nothing like that at all."

Perhaps this moral realignment is in part due to plagiarism charges levied against Tame Impala last year, or issues involving missing royalties, or the fact that he was able to set up his home studio thanks to the money he made from placing a song

in a BlackBerry commercial. It's all made Parker more willing to embrace making music for the masses: "If I could've had more conventional pop songs on this album, I would've."

While Parker can talk equipment or studio tactics for hours, he's much more reserved about his personal life. His father and mother divorced when he was three, and Parker grew up with his dad and stepmother in Perth, the fourth-biggest city in Australia. While his father dabbled in music—and was gifted with a Lennon-style singing voice—he also discouraged his son from doing it as a career, which led Parker to an unsuccessful and unfulfilling college stint studying engineering and astronomy. Although his father passed away before he began recording *Innerspeaker*, Parker says he admired the inherently sixties feel of the first Tame Impala EP.

As far as siblings, Parker says, "I have a full brother, a half sister, a half brother on the other side, a pretend sister, and … " I stop him right there—pretend sister? "My dad had a daughter in a marriage previous to my mom," he explains. "But he went to war in Africa for a few months and when he got back his wife was pregnant. Five years later, my dad started getting ransom-style notes at work saying, 'That's my daughter.' We got it checked out, and it turns out his wife had an affair while he was away at war, and it wasn't really his daughter." He pauses. "And my dad only told me when I was a teenager, so that's why she's a pretend sister."

Tame Impala burst out from relative obscurity with *Innerspeaker*, a vivid debut LP that built the bridge to the festival stages from which they now dispatch their wavy roar. That album brought about all of the touch points that a revivalist rock record could hope for: strong melody mixed with Blue Album Beatles psychedelia, tugging bass lines that gave the floaty music a little more weight, and a distinctly sharp drumming style that lent the music unexpected definition.

In an era of anonymous rock frontmen, *Innerspeaker* established Parker as an unlikely star, the type of musician who inspires imagination. His gear is cataloged and fawned over. His romantic life is tracked on a fairly lively SubReddit. He's sometimes heralded as the closest thing 2015 has to Jim Morrison, but in real life he's a sheepish dude who could probably be a case study in next week's "Rise of the Beta Males" think piece—a chill rock guy who is actually pretty stressed out about stuff he's not going to die from. Though his approach is studied and proprietary, he does not exactly radiate the sex-soaked intensity of a Rock God.

His second album, *Lonerism*, increased Tame Impala's scope without diminishing its returns and made it clear that Parker was gaining a better sense of himself as a producer and engineer. These songs felt deeper, thicker, and more assertive, even if the lyrics could be hopelessly vague. Parker sometimes likes to think of himself as more of an electronic producer and arranger than a rock musician, which makes sense given his trajectory thus far as well as the less riff-hungry sounds of *Currents*.

The new album feels more insular and personal while exuding a newfound sexiness, typified by the slow finger-snap funk of "'Cause I'm a Man." While Parker won't admit what he's made is good, per se—it's part humility on his part, part pathos of a serial perfectionist—he admits that his horizons stretched in ways that feel like gigantic leaps executed on a specific scale.

"I'm aware that there will be fans of my previous stuff for whom [*Currents*] doesn't resonate with as much, because they've got their values set," he says diplomatically. "But if I can convince a few die-hard rock fans that eighties synths can fit over a seventies drum beat—if I can help them to look outside the square of traditional psych rock—then at least one mission is accomplished."

At a Coachella warm-up show in the artsy enclave of Pomona, Tame Impala's typically unusual crowd shows up: college girls, old dudes with ponytails, a guy who works at a warehouse and is still wearing his Carhartt overalls. A teenager screams, "We need help! Someone just passed out!" and security guards reluctantly roll to the aid of some underage kids who got too fucked up, presumably on excitement and mushrooms. There's a lot of people wearing face glitter.

Everyone is revved up for the band, abandoning the conversations they carried on during the opening acts. The crowd loses its mind as a pitched-down version of Elton John's *Lion King* ode "Can You Feel the Love Tonight?" blasts from the PA and Tame Impala crawls onto the stage. Parker manages a "Who me?" wave as he unhinges his guitar from its stand. For a guy who's about to scorch the ceiling of a ballroom, he's loosey-goosey.

At one point, a bra floats up to the stage. Parker hangs it on a drum mic, and then, a few moments later, a thought hits him. "I almost forgot!" he calls out. "There was something written on it!" He nabs the bra.

"There's a phone number!" he exclaims. The entire room can feel him blush. ✍

Thanks for listening to Pitchfork Radio, live from Willys Detroit—Shinola's Midtown sister store.

Thanks to:
Peoples Records, WAYN Radio, David Hump, Ghostly International, Assemble Sound, Ben Christensen, Greg Baise, Hello Records, Tia Fletcher, Joey 2Lanes, Detroit Sound Conservancy, Aaron Siegel, Mike McGonigal, Brian Allnutt, Third Man Record, DJ Dan Kroha , Nat Morris, Scott Z, Duane The Teenage Weirdo, DJ Dave Buick, Protomartyr, V Count Macula, Matthew Dear, Aaron Siegel, Osborne DJ Dan Kroha, Jim Buelow

SHINOLA
DETROIT

Transfiguration & Transcendence

The Music of Alice Coltrane

BY ANDY BETA

ILLUSTRATIONS BY LAURA CALLAGHAN

Arespected yet divisive figure who was scorned by the jazz mainstream for most of her life, Alice Coltrane was one of the most complicated, and misunderstood of all twentieth-century musicians. In the twenty-first century, however, her music has grown in stature, and one can now hear echoes of her influence everywhere, from Björk's juxtaposition of timbres and textures to Joanna Newsom's harp playing, and from the twisted astral beats of Flying Lotus (her great-nephew Stephen Ellison) to the final works of her late husband John Coltrane. While his discography remains titanic in modern jazz, Alice's own albums are equally compelling and mysterious, suggesting a musical form that moves away from jazz and into a unique sonic realm that draws on classical Indian instrumentation, atonal modern orchestration, and homemade religious synth music. The adventurous nature and spiritual import of her work continues to resonate through New Age, jazz, and experimental electronic music of all stripes.

Alice used a number of names throughout her career, and collectively they chart a path of self-realization. The names she adopted demarcate radical shifts in her life and her work, serving effectively as chapter headings in the story of how a bebop pianist from Detroit evolved into one of jazz's singular visionaries, ultimately walking away from public performance to became a guru and beacon of enlightenment for others.

ALICE McLEOD

"There was such God feeling [in the church]. ... The pianist started playing at such a rapid pace, and everything just stopped. What could you do?" —from *The Monument Eternal: The Music of Alice Coltrane,* by Franya J. Berkman

Alice McLeod was born on August 27, 1937, in Alabama, though her family soon relocated to the rough east side of Detroit. The two world wars solidified Detroit's position as a manufacturing powerhouse and by 1959 it was the industrial center of the country. It had also gained renown as a bebop hot spot and was home to future jazz players like Cecil McBee, Donald Byrd, Paul Chambers, Milt Jackson, Yusef Lateef, Bennie Maupin, and Elvin Jones.

The McLeods were a musical family—Alice's mother, Anna, played in the church choir, her half brother Ernest Farrow was a prominent jazz bassist, and her sister Marilyn went on to be a songwriter at Motown— and Alice took up piano and organ at a young age. As a teen she accompanied Mt. Olive Baptist Church's three choirs, and at sixteen, she was invited to perform with the Lemon Gospel Singers during services at the more ecstatic Church of God in Christ (COGIC). In Franya J. Berkman's biography *Monument Eternal: The Music of Alice Coltrane,* Alice remembers those formative services as "the gospel experience of her life," an instance of devotional music that gave her teenage self "the experience of unmediated worship at the collective level."

Encouraged by her half brother Farrow, Alice continued to pursue music. She formed her own lounge act, performing gospel and R&B (with touches of blues and bebop) around Detroit. The young McLeod soon became a fixture of the city's jazz scene and found herself involved with Kenneth "Poncho" Hagood—a scat jazz singer who'd recorded with Thelonious Monk, Charlie Parker, and Miles Davis. The young couple were wed and relocated to Paris in the late fifties.

Alice gigged regularly around Paris, befriending other musicians like fellow pianist Bud Powell. In 1960, she gave birth to a daughter, Michelle—the joyousness of which was tempered by her husband's burgeoning heroin habit. It wasn't long before she returned to Detroit as a single mother, moved back in with her parents, and started picking up gigs to support her daughter. Once again immersed in the bustling Detroit scene, McLeod began to contemplate jazz beyond the dizzying array of chord changes, scales, and standards that were fundamental to the bop era. One album in particular spurred her creative contemplation: John Coltrane's *Africa/Brass*.

While known to be a junkie early in his career, by 1957 tenor saxophonist John Coltrane had kicked his habit and begun his musical ascent in earnest. He was a sideman for Thelonious Monk and in 1959 appeared on Miles Davis's modal masterwork, *Kind of Blue*. Coltrane was already an accomplished bandleader, releasing a slew of records from *Blue Train* (1957) to *My Favorite Things* (1961). Later that same year, firmly established as one of the greatest tenor saxophone players of his generation, he signed an exclusive recording contract with Impulse Records—the brand-new jazz imprint of producer Creed Taylor.

Coltrane's new deal allowed him the creative control and artistic freedom necessary to push jazz's boundaries and imagine new musical vistas. *Africa/Brass* was his first album for Impulse and featured a twenty-one-piece ensemble that included the preeminent reedman Eric Dolphy backed up by the rhythm section of pianist McCoy Tyner and drummer Elvin Jones. Cuts like "Africa"—an expansive suite augmented by birdcalls and jungle sounds—announce Coltrane as a tireless innovator, using Davis's modal template as the launching pad for new explorations.

Alice went to see John Coltrane and his new quartet when they played Detroit's Minor Key club in January of 1962. She didn't speak to Coltrane that night, but an opportunity to play piano in vibraphonist Terry Gibbs's ensemble brought her to New York City in the summer of 1963, where Gibbs's group opened for Coltrane's quartet during an extended engagement at Birdland. When her group wasn't on the bandstand, Alice was trying to work up the nerve to talk to Coltrane.

She describes her initial impressions in Berkman's book: "I had an inner feeling about him ... I was connecting with another message that I had perceived as coming through the music. At Birdland, that same feeling would come back, something that I comprehend was associated with my soul or spirit." The two musicians barely spoke, though Alice described Coltrane's silence as "loud." A few days later, still having exchanged very few words, Alice heard Coltrane playing a melody behind her. She turned and complimented him on its beautiful theme. He said it was for her.

ALICE COLTRANE

"Of course, John Coltrane is who inspires everybody, if you were fortunate enough to be in his presence in those days. He would always encourage you to express what you had ... You could hear your sound, music, light coming from the ethereal, heavenly realms."

John and Alice's relationship began in July of 1963, and they were married in Juarez, Mexico, in 1965. They remained together until his death from liver cancer two years later. Alice gave birth to their three sons: John Jr., Ravi, and Oran. While the couple only began to record together in February of 1966, their musical relationship spanned the duration of their romantic relationship, both predicated on mutual inspiration and spiritual elevation.

Alice had felt limited by the rigidity and orthodoxy of bebop throughout her career and, as her relationship with John bloomed, she found his influence on her musical explorations to be profound. The couple used musical innovation as a path toward personal enlightenment: "You heard all kinds of things that would have just been left alone, never a part of your discovery or appreciation." It's difficult to gauge the degree to which her approach to the piano changed once she met John, as aside from a few Terry Gibbs albums released in 1963 and 1964, few if any recordings of Alice's early performances exist. John Coltrane's discography from 1963 until 1967

demonstrates a restless urgency to expand every aspect of his horn and his music. Two Impulse albums from 1963 find Coltrane exploring ballads and collaborating with Duke Ellington and vocalist Johnny Hartman. While some critics see these albums as a response to being labeled "anti-jazz" by *Down Beat* in the early sixties, in hindsight they seem to serve as a reset and resting place—a last look back toward jazz history before Coltrane and his group forged ahead into an exploration of innovative new sounds.

At the end of 1964, Coltrane entered engineer Rudy Van Gelder's Englewood Cliffs studio in New Jersey with his classic quartet—pianist McCoy Tyner, bassist Jimmy Garrison, and thunderstorm drummer Elvin Jones—to record a four-part suite documenting a spiritual conversion he had undergone after an overdose almost ten years prior. "This album is a humble offering to Him," Coltrane wrote in the liner notes to *A Love Supreme*. "An attempt to say 'THANK YOU GOD' through our work." It's the summation of the quartet's lyrical, evocative, and dynamic power.

Within that same year the quartet would both expand (with the addition of second saxophonist Pharoah Sanders and second drummer Rashied Ali) and fray, with Tyner and Jones leaving. "All I could hear was a lot of noise," Tyner said in one interview. "I didn't have any feeling for the music." Starting in 1965, Coltrane embraced fiery free jazz—"the New Thing"—a sound that sought freedom from meter, chord changes, harmonies, and whatever else had previously defined and codified jazz. The influence of younger horn players like Sanders, Archie Shepp, and Albert Ayler on Coltrane is well documented, but very little has been said of the musician who replaced Tyner on the piano bench: Alice Coltrane.

Biographies of John Coltrane often reduce his marriage to a relationship between mentor and disciple, with John as the musical guru and Alice as the initiate. "Many of John Coltrane's fans viewed her as accomplice to the so-called anti-jazz experiments of his final years," Berkman writes, a sentiment that stemmed from "the controversial role she assumed when she replaced McCoy Tyner as pianist in her husband's final rhythm section." (Years later, Alice Coltrane contributed harp to Tyner's 1972 album *Extensions*.) Four years before Yoko Ono al-

legedly broke up the Beatles, thereby earning the scorn of all future generations of rock fans, Alice was accused of breaking up the greatest jazz group of the mid-sixties.

But Alice, if anything, was the catalyst for Coltrane's greatest music, abetting and inspiring his spiritual quest to realize a universal sound. When the couple met in 1963, Coltrane was still working within the framework of modal jazz. Soon after Alice entered his life, he started to push beyond the conventions of modern jazz, freeing himself from meter and steady tempo, fixed chord changes and melody. *A Love Supreme* was composed and realized after their relationship began. Seen in that light, the questing Coltrane albums *Ascension*, *Om*, *Meditations,* and more all stem from this relationship. Without Alice's own roots in the ecstatic spirit of the Church of God in Christ services and a shared interest in a less dogmatic and more universal understanding of God—to say nothing of their love and devotion to each other—would Coltrane's own spiritual transformation have occurred?

The Coltranes' spiritual study did not take place in a vacuum, but amid a broader religious upheaval and restructuring of the sixties. New forms of Afrocentric spirituality ranged from a renewed interest in Egyptology and the rituals of Santeria to Ron Karenga's creation of Kwanzaa (recognized in 1966) and the rise of the Nation of Islam. But Alice herself acknowledged that the new couple's pursuit intensified soon after they came together. "What we did was really begin to reach out and look toward higher experiences in spiritual life and higher knowledge," she told Berkman. Despite Alice's history in the church—with COGIC's direct experience of God through a communal, ecstatic music—and her subsequent life as a swamini, she still receives little acknowledgment in biographies and jazz history as catalyst for her husband's spiritual rebirth.

Alice herself didn't do much to correct these accounts. As the decade rolled along and music—as well as societal roles—became increasingly radicalized and questioned, Coltrane embraced her role as wife and mother. In a 1988 radio interview, she said of her marriage, "I didn't want to be equal to him. I didn't have to be equal to him and do what he did. That, I never considered. I don't think like that. And whatever in the women's liberation—that's what they want. I didn't want to be equal to him. I wanted to be a wife, to be ... that for him. To me, as a result of that association, it fully manifested. There was no more question about direction."

Once Alice joined her husband on the bandstand, they toured the world, the music going further and further out, with standards like "My Favorite Things" pushing toward the hour mark. Not that critics always noted her. In a February 23, 1967, *Down Beat* review of *Live at the Village Vanguard Again!*, Alice warrants but a single line in a fifteen-paragraph review: "Mrs. Coltrane's piano support is always firm and appropriate, never overbusy or obtrusive."

And then in May of 1967, John Coltrane complained of abdominal pain that was soon revealed to be liver cancer. By summer, he could no longer eat, and he left his earthly body on July 17, 1967.

ALICE TURIYA COLTRANE

"I hope to be able to do some of the work thought of by John, with recordings, concerts and whatever community work, but there is a higher and culminating idea in the mind of John, which I hope will become a reality during my lifetime." —from the liner notes to A Monastic Trio, 1968

The names she adopted demarcate radical shifts in her life and her work, serving effectively as chapter headings in the story of how a bebop pianist from Detroit evolved into one of jazz's singular visionaries.

In quick succession, Alice Coltrane suffered the loss of both her husband and her half brother Ernest Farrow. Her account of her spiritual awakening between 1968 and 1970 in her self-published tract, *Monument Eternal,* is harrowing: her weight plunged from 118 to 95 pounds and her family worried for her well-being. In her telling, her weight loss was not the result of grief and depression but due to *tapas*—extreme austerities undertaken for spiritual advancement. It leads to detached remembrances, like: "During an excruciating test to withstand heat, my right hand succumbed to a third-degree burn. After watching the flesh fall away and the nails turn black, it was all I could do to wrap the remaining flesh in a linen cloth."

The rainbow-covered booklet makes no mention of her jazz music career, her husband, or her travels to India. Instead, she matter-of-factly details making a doctor recoil in horror at the sight of her blackened flesh, what occurs when one experiences supreme consciousness, the nuances of various astral planes, her ability to hear trees sing, and scaring the family dog with her astral projections. Amid this, her family feared for her sanity: "My relatives became extremely worried about my mental and physical health. Therefore they arranged for my return to their home for 'care and rest.'" Later she adds: "Communicating with people was found to be like suffering judgment. In fact, it was almost impossible for me to dwell upon earthly matters, and equally impossible for me to bring the mind down to mundane thoughts and general conversations."

Deep in this quest, Alice assumed control of her husband's formidable estate and released his first posthumous album in September 1967, *Expression*. And while *Down Beat* gave it four stars, Don DeMichael wrote: "Mrs. Coltrane, while sounding somewhat like McCoy Tyner, does not have her predecessor's physical or musical strength." She soon after released her first album as leader, *A Monastic Trio* (1968). On it, she referred to her husband by her spiritual name for him, Ohnedaruth ("compassion"), and sought to follow his example to create a music that was free, open-ended, and spiritually questing. The album features late-period quartet bandmates Pharoah Sanders, Jimmy Garrison, and Rashied Ali, with Alice on piano as well as a new instrument for her, harp.

Alice's self-taught playing style on harp—ordered for her by her husband, who didn't live to see its arrival—was full of glissandi and accentuated arpeggios and took cues from another Detroiter, Dorothy Ashby, but Coltrane's playing was decidedly more abstract. She compared the piano to a sunrise and the harp to a sunset, marveling at "the subtleness, the quietness, the peacefulness" of the latter instrument. It would figure prominently in her future albums. Such subtlety was lost on critics at the time, with *Down Beat's* review of *A Monastic Trio* labeling Alice's playing as "a wispy impressionist feeling without urgent substance."

Fans and critics expecting the strength and urgency in her husband's music were befuddled by Alice Coltrane's approach as a bandleader. *Down Beat* wrote of one album: "It seems incredible that a group so heavily stamped by the late John Coltrane would not be able to pull off an album, but that's just what happens here." As more posthumous John Coltrane albums came to market, some featuring Alice's own harp and string arrangements on top of previously recorded sessions, critics were enraged by the perceived blasphemy.

"Black female musicians have been quintessential others, overlooked because of ... gender, race and class," Berkman writes. "Black female musicians rarely transcend difference and obtain the status of artist." In the context of such overt racism and sexism, Alice's early solo albums were at odds not only with jazz's "New Thing"—chaotic free-blowing sessions that roared and shrieked for entire sides of vinyl—but also with late-sixties radicalism and black power. At a time when African American female artists from Abbey Lincoln to Nina Simone were growing more and more politically outspoken, when riots and protests were roiling the inner cities of America, Alice's music was the diametric opposite of such trends: introspective and contemplative, gentle and impressionistic.

Cecil McBee, a jazz bassist who played with Alice at the turn of the decade, says of her position and approach: "Where we were trying to come from [as free jazz musicians], with the loudness and bombast of our music, she made these statements in a more delicate, graceful, articulate, and uniform way than we did." She was intentionally making something softer than protest music; she wasn't demonstrating on the bandstand. In an era when national, racial, and gender identity were highly contentious, Alice Coltrane was aiming for transcendence.

The Coltranes' universalist view, which dates back to *A Love Supreme*, came into focus for Alice Coltrane in 1969 when she was introduced to a figure who clarified her spiritual path and resolve, Swami Satchidananda. Invited to New York City by film director Conrad Rooks, Swami Satchidananda came to visit in 1967 and began to lecture at the Unitarian Universalist Church in the Upper West Side, soon establishing the first Integral Yoga Institute on West End Avenue. Within a few years, Satchidananda made the spread in *Life* magazine's Year of the Guru issue and then sold out Carnegie Hall. He later opened the ceremonies at Woodstock. Alice gravitated to his Eastern philosophy of self-knowledge and became close friends with the Swami.

Anticipating a trip to accompany the Swami through India, Alice Coltrane entered the studio in 1970 to record what is arguably the most sumptuous spiritual jazz album of the era, *Journey in Satchidananda*. The liner notes speak of that upcoming voyage, but the music itself reveals that a stunning internal shift has already occurred, fitting for the cryptic title, in that "Satchidananda" is not an external destination to be journeyed to, but rather a place to be discovered within. Augmented by oud, tamboura, Sanders's soprano saxophone, and McBee's bowed bass, Coltrane's assured harp playing takes on a Technicolor vibrancy, entwining with Indian overtones to create a divine music that transcends not only the limitations of jazz but of both Eastern and Western music, and anticipates the rise of New Age music at its most resonant.

McBee described the sessions to Berkman as intimate: "It was very, very spiritual. The lights would be low and she had incense and there was not much conversation ... about what was to be. The spiritual, emotional, physical statement of the environment, it was just there. You felt it and you just played it." The month after *Satchidananda* was released, Alice accompanied the Swami to India for a five-week trip, visiting New Delhi, Ceylon (now Sri Lanka), Rishikesh, and Madras. She brought her harp with her, an exotic sight to most Indians, and also began to learn Hindu devotional hymns.

Alice returned from the pilgrimage and recorded her next album, *Universal Consciousness*, shortly thereafter. It deftly mixes orchestral strings, Indian timbres, harp, and the Wurlitzer organ, an instrument Alice said had been revealed to her in a vision. It was a music she described as a "Totality concept, which embraces cosmic thought as an emblem of Universal Sound." And while a fellow devotee of Indian music, George Harrison, might have set Hindu chants to folk-rock arrangements, Alice saw in them something both avant-garde and transcendent. One won't mistake her version of "Hare Krishna"—with a harp and orchestral arrangement that could levitate mountains—for what you hear chanted in Union Square. Even *Down Beat* couldn't deny its majesty, calling *Universal Consciousness* a "paragon of the new music. ... [Alice] emerged as the strongest of Coltrane's disciples. Her leadership affects everyone, consequently producing a stunningly beautiful result."

That adoration was short-lived in the press, with her last two albums for Impulse getting dismissive reviews. *World Galaxy* earned two and a half stars, lambasted as "super-saccharine, often corny and terribly repetitive," while *Lord of Lords* was described as being "not much more than pretty music ... made up of little more than strung-together arpeggios and glissandi ... a massive swaying smear."

For Alice's great-nephew, Flying Lotus, the turbulent and beautiful *Lord of Lords* goes far deeper: "For me, that record is the story of John Coltrane's ascension. It's her understanding and coping with his death. In particular, 'Going Home,' that's a family song. When someone passes, that's the song we play at the funeral. When my auntie passed, we played that one. When my mom died, we played it for her." Some thirty years after its performance, it was turned back into a gospel hymn by a former student of his and entitled "Going Home." In performing it, Coltrane paid tribute to her parents' favorite church hymn. *Lord of Lords* would be her last release on Impulse Records.

SWAMINI A.C. TURIYASANGITANANDA

"I got ready and put on a white dress and all, and I noticed when the time came, the colors of orange were poured into the cloth of the dress I was wearing ... I just

watched everything go into that beautiful saffron color."
—from the last interview with Alice Coltrane, 2006

In 1976, Alice Coltrane received a divine message to start an ashram and renounced the secular, beginning her new life clad in the orange robes of the Swamini. And while there were a few more studio albums for Warner Bros., the music contained within for the most part no longer consisted of original compositions but rather iterations of Indian hymns. Beginning on her first trip to India, Alice began to adapt *bhajans*—the Indian hymns associated with the Bhakti revival movement of India—to be sung at worship services at the ashram. Her last two WB albums, *Radha-Krsna Nama Sankirtana* and *Transcendence* (both released in 1977), comprised such devotional music, and soon after, she no longer performed in public or recorded for a label. A few years later, a series of four albums was self-released on cassette: *Turiya Sings* (1982), *Divine Songs* (1987), *Infinite Chants* (1990), and *Glorious Chants* (1995). The music within reveals a private universe of cosmic contemplation, the Swamini accompanying herself on electric organ, sometimes with her students chanting along with her. It's a disarming music, both solemn and celebratory, haunting yet joyous.

When she removed herself from the material world to devote herself to more spiritual matters later that same decade, writing four books about her divine revelations, she was called Swamini Turiyasangitananda by her devoted students, an eight-syllable name that translates from Hindi as "the Transcendental Lord's highest song of bliss." Coming into prominence in an era when almost every rock star and jazz musician dabbled in Eastern mysticism and wrapped themselves in spiritual clothing only to drop them later, Alice Coltrane embodied that change wholly, turning away from public acclaim and becoming a Hindu swamini and teacher.

As a child, Flying Lotus visited Alice at the ashram every Sunday: "It's a very beautiful place, very musical. After my aunt would speak, she would play music. She'd be on the organ and people would bring instruments and there would be singing and chanting. The sounds Auntie would get out of that organ were *crazy*. I still never heard anyone play like that. It was super funky. As a kid, I didn't have an appreciation for it. Now I have a different perspective on it." Ellison told me that as a

young teenager, he traveled to India with his aunt and witnessed strangers on the street drop to their knees to kiss her feet, realizing her divine presence.

To get to the Sai Anantam Ashram, one must drive through the entire length of the San Fernando Valley, toward the Pacific Ocean and the Santa Monica Mountains, before turning down a road that winds through Agourra Hills, the land brown and red with tufts of white and green brush. Past a vineyard and an equestrian center, there is a dirt road to the ashram's gate, which is open to the public for only four hours each Sunday. The grounds are almost silent.

On a bright Sunday afternoon in August, there are only eight people at the Vedantic Center's service. Plastic patio chairs line the walls of the unadorned room and marigold throw pillows are scattered throughout atop plush royal-blue carpet. The devotees, clad all in white, sit still yet sing with great fervor. Music fills the room; led by an organist situated between garlanded portraits of Sai Baba and Swamini Turiyasangitananda, the gathered sing more than a dozen hymns, accompanied by organ and the hand drums, bells, and rattles that the devotees play themselves. The bhajans segue into one another, and, curiously, these Indian hymns have a Pentecostal gospel feel to them, the blues coursing through each mesmerizing movement to suggest a place where Southeast Asia and the Deep South of America meet.

After the two-hour service is concluded, the small congregation gathers for fellowship. Since the Swamini's passing on January 12, 2007, only seven people live at the ashram. Over carrot-raisin bread and a paper cup of strawberry lemonade from Trader Joe's, the remaining devotees of Turiyasangitananda discuss the upcoming anniversary of their Swamini's passing. The word *death* is not used. One member says that they should no longer call it a "memorial," as that word lingers on the past. Another offers up a suggestion: the anniversary should be called an ascension, as a way to keep the blessed Swamini Alice Coltrane Turiyasangitananda forever in the present. ✍

ANDY BETA *listens and writes widely. He explores electronic music with his* Electric Fling *column, and previously he wrote an appreciation of Texas soul singer Joe Tex for the* Pitchfork Review.

X-Offenders

A Typical Day in the Life of an NYC Proto-Punk

1976

BY LISA JANE PERSKY

WITH GARY VALENTINE. PHOTO BY JIMMY DESTRI

1966

Depending on where you're from, you might call this place squalid. There are roaches and sometimes a rat bouncing through last night's spaghetti sauce and eating your soap, but people sign up for it on purpose— and then they stuff steel wool in the rat holes to keep 'em out—because art is happening all the time. Art and crime. But that doesn't mean artists are criminals, does it? It's hard to tell.

I move into 87 Christopher Street, a prewar tenement building between Bleecker and Sheridan Square, in the middle of the night with my mother and stepfather, three dogs, and three semi-sibs, ages two, one, and none. I was eleven. We'd lived other places in Greenwich Village but this place was us dropping in after a high point, and on the downslide for what was the longest stay of all.

It's my urban bonanza, wild outpost on the edge of a new frontier. I am the girl with the records and the record player. I am the kid. My stepfather practices his violin every day, sometimes with the apartment door open with accompaniment by Yoko Ono herself shrieking at her husband (our super) until the police finally come. Maybe she's just tuning up, finding her sound. I see John Cage around Bank Street, Jimi Hendrix on Sixth Avenue. They remind me: I am the girl who listens.

Time and people move on and we take over three contiguous apartments in that building of only twenty. We take them over with the dream of connecting each by a spiral stair. The building also hosts actors, dancers, a playwright, an antiquarian book collector, old nesting-doll immigrant ladies who live together, an old man who jumped ship to avoid I don't know what, an even older man looking for the person who put a box in his throat that makes him scream "Motherfucking Yankee bastards!" in the hall. We are Puerto Rican, Costa Rican, Greek, black, Italian, southern, straight and homosexual, Catholics, agnostics, atheists and Jews. There's political action, radical feminism, music, dance, judo, ecology and burlap. There was/is Fluxus, *The Vagina Painting, Morning Piece*, and *Let There Be Neon*. There are plays on the rooftop and fire escape, and, finally, the barely portable Sony Portapak to capture whatever might happen or be invented out of what happens. We feel advanced. Ubiquitous views of my magical teenage years include many transvestites in golden jewels and sequined dresses, buff asses in chaps and chains, musicians in Washington Square.

That thing with the spiral staircase never happens, but in June of '73, I rent one of the three apartments for myself. The monthly seventy-five bucks isn't easy to make but two days after my last one as a high school senior, I'm walking up our block when my favorite denizen of number 87—resident Greek Chorus leader and playwright H.M. Koutoukas—sidles up to me. He's swishing like (to quote himself about himself) a washing machine and he says, "Dar-*LING*, I've written a play for you! Rehearsal starts Sunday at La Mama. The pay is twenty-five dollars a week. I'm sending someone to pick you up." After his proclamation, he parks me in front of our building to watch him agitate westward toward the sun as it sinks into the Hudson, beyond the collapsing piers. Harry, as friends and fellows call him, is the author of a play titled *Awful People Are Coming Over So We Must Be Pretending to Be Hard at Work and Hope They Will Go Away.*

IN NEW YORK, 1976. PHOTO BY GARY VALENTINE

The title of the play supposedly written for me is *Grandmother Is in the Strawberry Patch* and my role is Cordelia Wells, the World's Most Perfect Teenager. Thus begins my relationship with East Fourth Street and the Bowery.

I make sweeps of CBGB's early on, beginning with poetry readings, where I perform a few times with bums, drunks, and a few other open-mic'ers. There are serious poets here but I do not include myself among them. This is the neighborhood venue so whoever's been in the neighborhood—even for a night—has just shown up for whatever they did or whatever there was, including an actual hobo's soliloquy, "Riding the Rails," which contained only one line repeated over and over for eight minutes: "Ridin' the rails pickin' peaches, pickin' peaches, pickin' peaches ... " No one left the room. Plus, all the straight boys I know are in bands and since the collapse of the Mercer Arts Center they're all drifting this way.

January 1976

I start off the year rehearsing another play on East Fourth Street. This one is called *Women Behind Bars*. I'm dating a guy I met through my friend Lance Loud—of the first-ever reality teevee show, *An American Family*—and frontman for the band the Mumps. I'm looking for "the one" because everyone around here keeps asking me who my *real* boyfriend is. New Guy works for MainMan, has a Pollenex handheld showerhead, amenities I've never heard of, and gave me a test pressing of Bowie's *Station to Station* days before its release, but we have nothing else in common. I can't love him because he thinks it will be cute if we get matching pajamas, because he's a grown-up, and worse, he lives uptown.

Lance and I share a passion for guys. Last year he tried to fix me up with Robert Palmer but *no*. We did not even like each other a little. Lance may still be pissed at me because his childhood friend and Mumps drummer Jay Dee left the band last year to play with Patti Smith. According to Lance, Jay told him that I'd thought it was the best idea for everyone. What? Maybe he used me to take the heat off of himself or maybe Lance made this

up. I don't know. Jay made his own decision, the right thing for him—but it left the Mumps first in chaos and then in limbo.

But Lance can't stay mad at me for long. I'm the only person he knows that lives on Christopher Street. My place is the pit stop on the way to and from the boy Paradise. I'm also a real record-listening buddy. We zone to Odetta, Lewis Furey, Leadbelly, Sparks, and Jobriath together. We even share whaling songs, and I just wrote the first review of the Mumps for a new paper that's about to hit the streets and clubs called *New York Rocker*.

Alongside *Station to Station*, other records that suffer punishing groove wear at home are *The Modern Lovers*, *John Lennon/Plastic Ono Band*, John Cale's *Fear*, and Patti Smith's *Horses*—not just because of Patti, but because of what having a band and Cale have done for her, for us. "Tower bells chimed." Yes. We like *Birdland*, and not least of all, Blondie.

Blondie bassist and X-Offender songwriter Gary Valentine entered my life in the same way that acting did. Benton Quin, the "somebody" that H.M. Koutoukas had sent to pick me up for the play, the actor who had played Eunice, the Woman Next Door, had become the landlord of what's now known as "the Blondie Loft" at 266 Bowery. He'd invited Chris and Debbie to live there and along with them came their new bandmates: Clem, Gary, and then Jimmy.

In the spring of 1975, Benton called me and said, "I've got *someone* for you." I was skeptical but also optimistic, diligent. I went over. Gary and I hang out a lot, read comics together, talk about art, music, and books. He's part delinquent, part thinker, and so I like him right away but I'm recovering from a breakup, seeing other people. There's a photographer in another Bowery loft down the street, a guy from my acting class who works in a hospital as a flesh retainer, Rob duPrey, also of the Mumps, and it goes on like this. I'm a butterfly and I can't land. We're all pissed to have discovered the Love Generation to be a sham but we're still hopping around bed to bed like no one's going to get hurt, because we're so goddamn young. And there are so many cute boys and girls.

But it gets to be fall and all over piss-poor New York,

people are running out of money for oil for heat, for hot water. This fact forges relationships by necessity. Sometimes you have to bathe at someone else's place. In my apartment, the bathtub is in the kitchen and semiprivate, meaning no one can see you if no one is there. Eventually, Gary comes over for a bath. Benton is right. "One magical moment, such is the stuff from where dreams are woven." According to *Phonograph Record* magazine we are the downtown Lancelot and Guinevere.

Gary moves into 87 Christopher Street. And we are clean. Very clean. And we have arrived at our particular day:

December 23, 1976

We get up at 6:30 (having recently gone to bed), get dressed, and jump on the IRT at Sheridan Square. Today we're going to try a last-minute part-time temp job because we always need more money. This one's a staple for the unskilled: envelope stuffing. We assume we'll have a knack for it. The office is near the World Trade Center. The last time we were down here we came to see King Kong the robot monster ape on the day they filmed his terrible demise, because we love robots and monsters and apes. Turned out he was a very popular ape. Thirty thousand other people showed up, too. It was June and so warm.

We hike up the stairs of the building on lower Broadway, go down a long green hall, find and open the office door. It's a closet: an actual closet. No window. One table with ten other schmucks like us sitting at it. "All too damned grateful to get this job." Boxes and boxes of envelopes, stacks of papers to be folded and stuffed, and quiet as a grave. We stuff 'n' fold for two of the four hours under my nemesis, the fluorescent light. I feel clammy, run to find the bathroom, and have the most heartfelt dry heave of my life. When I come back, I only have to look at Gary to understand that we're both done here.

We apologize, backing out through the door of that joint "smiling and waving and looking so fine," running all the way to the loft, kicking over trash cans and karate-chopping air because we have to show even the invisible enemy that we are invincible. It's so—*punk*—which is a word we're refusing to associate ourselves or friends with. We just feel alive, connected, invulnerable.

We hang out in the main room of the loft, smoking butts from an ashtray, still wearing our coats, burning hand-screened Jimi Hendrix posters in the fireplace to get warm. These lovely gems were left by a former tenant but we don't save shit. We're on the move, living in closets. We have no money to buy anything and no place to keep it.

WITH GARY VALENTINE IN A PLAYLAND PHOTO BOOTH

We know we're lucky.
We like being us.

Everyone else in the loft is still asleep, balled up like cats. Sometimes when Chris and Debbie get up, Debbie makes eggs for us. Chris tokes up and can occasionally boss us around. We call them Ike and Tina. They seem so married and a bit fuddy-duddy to us but they're also warm and parental, they share. Chris gets a steady check from the government that is referred to as "nut money" because he's nuts, supposedly. We admire his chops with the bureaucracy. Most everyone we know has some grift going. If you're a good enough guy you're running the scam that does the least damage to others; if you're a good enough girl, you run the scam that hurts only you.

Last night Benton and I stole a Christmas tree. We think it was meant to be taken but we didn't ask to find out, just snuck off with it. It has branches on one side only and it was on the very end of the row so we grabbed this little busted-up pine and took off around the corner—and I kept going until I got it to my apartment. Gary and I turned the bad side to the wall, tied it to the heat pipe so it would stand up straight, dressed it up like a rock star. Even though *Station to Station* stands as the "it" record at our place, we're still living *Hunky Dory*.

It's one P.M. and I run for the Chelsea Hotel, where my next job is. There's a Blondie gig at CB's tonight so Gary stays at the loft plucking the unamplified strings of his guitar until everyone wakes up or arrives for rehearsal. As much as we are happy, in love, and there is still the feeling that we could "float among the stars together, [he] and I," I never know if someone will take my place as soon as we're apart. There are girls in every nook and cranny looking to sweep up your cute boyfriend no mat-

ter who you are or who he is, even if they already have cute boyfriends of their own. And this is not even counting the groupies who have accumulated this year. Women's Lib might as well be short for Women's Libido. Many are vicious girls looking for a fight. Some even cut one another—not me, but when I have to, I look like I would.

I've worked at the Chelsea off and on since 1973—not for the hotel but for Charles James, a legendary couturier, a seventy-year-old genius that few remember. He's done himself in with his uncompromising perfectionism. It made him bitter and he's scraping by on the good graces of a few loyal and loaded patrons. I got this job by recommendation from Koutoukas again, my guardian angel. For the moment, he and Alan Betrock, editor and publisher of *New York Rocker*, seem to have answered the question of what it is that I do, but when Charles calls, I'm here. I'm walking Sputnik, his dog, I'm collating his archive for the Smithsonian Institute. I'm typing a tome of an angry letter to Halston, whom Charles accuses of ripping everyone off.

I love this job, in spite of Charles's manic tendencies. He takes time out from his work to teach me about the poetry of Rupert Brooke and Hart Crane and the music of Debussy and about perfumes and classic fit and line, the author/photographer Carl Van Vechten and Leopold and Loeb, and he tells me amazing stories about his life. He also pays me on time even when he's going to be late with his rent. Since it's hard for the hotel's famous bastard manager Stanley Bard to say no to a young girl—or maybe just me—I plead Charles's case on my way out. In spite of Bard's horrible reputation he can be sympathetic.

I can't love him because he thinks it will be cute if we get matching pajamas, because he's a grown-up, and worse, he lives uptown.

Claude Lelouche is in the hotel, and Peter Brook and I see Leonard Cohen come and go. People leave their doors open and you hear a lot of bad guitar and even saxophone in the hall and wild people are always bitching and trying to get away with something at the front desk. And if we're not yet already, we all *know* we're going to be *somebody*.

I earn my $1.50 an hour but I always feel guilty taking money from Charles.

It's 5:30 and I'm walking down Seventh Avenue toward home, saving this money for cab fare for tonight. Art Pepper's always around, playing the Village Vanguard. Tonight he seems to give me a little nod (or was he nodding? I'm not sure).

When I get home, Gary's high school buddy and fellow Blondie, Clem Burke, is leaving our apartment. He sometimes comes by, fresh off the PATH train at Christopher Street, to bake his hair in our oven. He turns it on low, gets on his knees, and sticks his head in there,

turning gently side to side to get his proper Eric–of–Bay City Rollers height and volume.

We all have our quirks, for sure. Gary and I iron all of our clothes except T-shirts and underwear. We wear the same pegged pants and white button-down collared shirts from the Salvation Army in Hoboken and skinny ties like the Beatles circa 1966.

Tonight Blondie's playing CBGB's with the Mumps and debuting a song that Gary and I wrote together. It's called "Euphony"—wordplay meant to imply *You Phony*. The pop sensibility that most of the bands embrace—not unlike the tenor of *Women Behind Bars*—includes puns, tongue-in-cheek humor, and blatant references to old movies, music, and art.

Written by Tom Eyen (now of *Dreamgirls* renown), *Women Behind Bars* is a spoof of overwrought 1950s women's prison films. It's also a somewhat loving, camp homage to the old Women's House of Detention that was on Greenwich Avenue, halfway between 87

GARY VALENTINE IN THE BLONDIE LOFT. PHOTO BY LISA JANE PERSKY

BACKSTAGE AT *WOMEN BEHIND BARS*. PHOTO BY ELLIE SCHADT

Christopher and where Tom Eyen lives on West Tenth. They tore it down a couple of years ago and all that's left is an empty lot behind the Jefferson Market Library.

On the nights that Gary and I both work on the East Side, he walks me to the theater and then convenes at the loft with the rest of the band. We split from 87 and head across Bleecker Street at 6:30. This gives us time to down a hot slice at Amalfi Pizza and pick up a bag of bones from Ottamanelli's Meat Market on the other side of Seventh Avenue. These bones are stand-ins in the play. The Matron's assistant, Louise (played by Sweet William Edgar), tosses the black Hefty bag containing them onto the floor with a clunk and the Matron (played by Divine) says, "What *is it,* Louise?" and Louise says, "It's *the Harvey Girls*," to which Divine replies with a shudder, "Oh yeah, I forgot about them."

When the Harvey Girls work up a good stench, I'm responsible for a new load-a dem bones. You just can't fake that sound.

As we cross Sixth Avenue still along Bleecker Street headed east, the Hare Krishnas are carrying on with their hare hare rama rama Krishna, Krishna hare fuckin' hares, and we're so over it, just like we're over disco. We wear Death to Disco buttons now, not because we never liked it or never danced (I go to the Limelight and Gary and I go to Club 82) but because it's been years of this already.

In the play, I'm "the Innocent, Raped by the System." I'm also faux-raped in high camp style by Divine and the inmates. We're performing at the Truck and

Warehouse Theater, which is across the street from La Mama—where I did the Koutoukas play—and the aforementioned outré Club 82. We do eight shows a week and all of the bone-chilling hijinks occur at breakneck speed—an hour and ten minutes flat if it's going well. All the local bands have been to the play at least once. Craig Gholson of *New York Rocker* brought David Byrne a second time because, he says, David has a crush on me. I don't know if he's kidding but I'm sooo creeped out by it that I can't make eye contact with Byrne for years. People go to the shows to watch David spazz out on "Psycho Killer" and bawk like a chicken. He moves like an unrehearsed version of the skeletons in a Betty Boop cartoon. Bones again. It's not sexy.

Elton John comes to the play whenever he's in New York. He buys a whole row and brings his entourage. He and Divine become friends and he asks Divine to be in his upcoming Madison Square Garden Show. He gives the rest of the cast our own row of seats and we all go. It's "Don't Go Breakin' My Heart" time with Kiki Dee and then Divine comes out shakin' that thing and at once is exposed to more people than in all the screenings of *Pink Flamingos* put together. The crowd goes crazy. When Divine is sick or does another gig, one of her two understudies is Holly Woodlawn, the other is Monti Rock III (aka Disco Tex of Disco Tex and the Sexelettes). Tom Waits shoots the album cover for *Small Change* in our dressing room.

After the play I *have* to see Suicide. It's 9:30 and I'm cabbing it to Max's Kansas City for their first set. I'm obsessed, even though I'm not sure I "get" what it is they are. No one's ever there. Fifteen people at the most. They don't care. They're going to do the most amazing, earnest, in-your-face show whether you come or not. Suicide is not like anything else. Marty sets up his rig behind Alan. They perform in minimal light. Alan cuts himself at compelling moments in the music. He tells me it's no big deal. He knows how to do it so he'll heal fast. Marty's at his most dynamic in front of an audience and tells me that now when he's not onstage, he's just killing time until he gets there, that he wears the sunglasses for privacy. I ask him what he thinks of what Alan's doing up there. "I haven't seen Alan for years," he says. Alan and Marty forever. Nothing compares. Sure, everyone wants a contract, but not everyone will change to get one.

I cab it to CB's hoping to get there in time for the second sets so I can see Gary and Debbie sing "Euphony." Roberta lets me in. I never check anything at the door, though. My "Little Johnny Jewel" single got pinched from there. CBGB's isn't just for friends anymore; it's jammed with kids from the boroughs, Long Island, and New Jersey. Every band has their following and fanbase of strangers. Manager-slash-label guys are prowling the place. Unsigned groups are in the throes of second-guessing themselves in hopes of getting a contract. They're making changes or maybe mistakes.

The good times are over but it's still a great night for Blondie. When the last guitar is packed, we move on to the sidewalk, hang out in front for as long as Gary and I can stand the cold, then, bending our bodies against the freezing wind, we strike out for home and our Christmas tree. We talk about my show, his shows, various people and their bullshit, their drug habits, about our favorite bands: Television, Suicide, Heartbreakers, Ramones, Mumps, Miamis, the Fast, Marbles, Talking Heads. We know we're lucky. We like being us.

We can already sense that once the money flows and careers kick into gear, the magic that Koutoukas calls "the Ancient Laws of Glitter" will recede from our grasp, but this is our music now, the foot on the prewar stair, the unlocking of locks and slamming of doors, the banging and clanging of pipes, running water, the wail of babies, fights from the other side of the wall, the sirens and honking of horns, dishes clattering in the sink, people hollering back and forth from street to window, window to street, the rattle and squeal of the subway, the hiss of kettles and radios and of television sets at three A.M., the sounds of hoots and wolf whistles, of bongo players across the air shaft, trucks roaring over the cobblestones of Seventh Avenue, sounds of the ordinary, the damaged, the exalted, the insane. We'll have to listen more carefully now for our instincts, for our art, to connect again to the music that is this life. Today is Gary's birthday and we'd better fall asleep before the sun comes up. Later on we're going to see *King Kong* in Times Square. ✐

LISA JANE PERSKY *is a founding staff member of the* New York Rocker *and* Los Angeles Review of Books. *Among others, she has contributed to* Mojo, *the* L.A. Times, Journal of Popular Music Studies. *She has appeared on, off, and off-off Broadway and in numerous television shows and films.*

Lone Wolf Like Me

Tunde and Carvell on Being a Long Ways from Home

BY CARVELL WALLACE

ILLUSTRATIONS BY MARIA INES GUL

A NOTE FROM CARVELL

When I was young, my mother and I used to steal videos from a store in North Hollywood. She would check them out and never return them. After a significant amount of time had passed, she would send me in to explain—in my most genial and convincing tone—that they had been accidentally misplaced. The owners would relent, rent us another, and we'd do the same thing. It took about a year for us get banned. This is how I came to watch *Jesus Christ Superstar*, *She's Gotta Have It*, and *Purple Rain* each about three hundred times in a row.

When I was in LA to interview TV On The Radio's Tunde Adebimpe, I drove by the store and discovered that it was, improbably, still in business. It had somehow managed to outlast Blockbuster and even the Tower on Ventura where I had my first job. It made me laugh. I immediately thought to text my mother and tell her, maybe even take a picture. She would think it was funny. It was a good two seconds before it occurred to me that my mother had died. Seven years ago. In my arms. From lung cancer. What followed this realization was a feeling of isolation unlike any I had ever known, suddenly and completely enveloping me, seemingly from out of nowhere. Out of the sky. It was so visceral, so all-encompassing, and so sudden that sobs escaped my chest and filled up the rental car while I waited for the light to change.

The light turned green and I kept driving. It was over as suddenly as it had started. South down Vineland Avenue. Noticing how, no matter what you're feeling, the sun always looks so hopeful and sad in the late California afternoon.

Both Tunde and I grew up as the only black person around white people, which means that both of us have practiced for decades how to walk the delicate line between authenticity and connection, between telling the truth and being safe.

I met Tunde sometime in the mid-nineties while we were both students at an overwhelmingly white art school. I remember noticing his awkward, tall gait and the fact that he wore the same kind of musty black band T-shirts I did. Mostly I remember that we both wore the same hat every day. It seems like a little thing now, but it has always struck me as a particular kind of nineties black-freak symbolism. You're forming a fledgling style designed to set you apart, but being a kid you don't really know basic adult-man etiquette like don't wear the same hat every day because it will smell. You are forming an identity that is dependent on communicative accessories (perhaps more than is necessary). You need everyone to know that you're cool, or different. Quirky. The hat represents how you want to be seen. It is important. Because without it, you might look like just another black kid.

And you know how everyone treats "just another black kid."

Eventually, after nodding what's-up around the halls a handful of times, we started talking. I don't remember what we said to each other, but I'm sure it was a lot of unspecific bro speak about Hendrix or whatever, punctuated by "right on," "totally," and awkward pauses. I remember feeling like I had maybe finally met someone I could connect to. Another black dude who knew the entire Sonic Youth and Bad Brains catalog. Who wouldn't tease me for not being able to dance, or for smoking the wrong brand of cigarette. A lone wolf like me. This should have been a relief, but it wasn't. In retrospect, it was terrifying.

I remember him giving me his number as we stood outside a campus building on Broadway smoking hand-rolled cigarettes. "We should hang out," he said.

"Totally," I said.

But, of course, I never called him.

Almost two decades later I was dispatched to interview Tunde. He was now a bona fide rock star, a name and voice people knew. I wasn't sure if he remembered how I flaked on our would-be friendship. I brought it up when we finally made good on our promise to hang out some eighteen years later under an oak tree in Griffith Park. He laughed.

"If only you knew I was just an isolated animator literally starving for human contact," he said.

It occured to me as I interviewed him that there was a fundamental difference between us: we suffered the same isolation, but we dealt with it entirely differently. My loneliness was terminal and made it impossible for me to create. His loneliness was superseded only by his desire to create. He made work because making work was the one thing he didn't doubt.

Reading back the transcript of the interview, I'm struck by how hard it is for either of us to say anything plainly to each other. Our sentences are characterized by frequent pauses, clauses, clarifications, and rephrasing. We rarely utter a complete thought. We use generalized terms designed to minimize misunderstandings or offense. We issue retractions for things we haven't even said yet. It is almost as though we're slightly afraid of each other.

This may have to do with what we have in common. Having black skin but liking white things is a little like walking on a tightrope: it is a very limited way of being. You have white friends with whom you can never talk about race but you avoid groups of black people because you fear they will hear what's in your headphones and call you out as a traitor or an Uncle Tom. You just want to be able to listen to your Siouxsie tapes in peace and you are afraid of anything that might upset that—and everything might upset that. So you form a loving relationship with isolation. With loneliness. You are like a motherless child.

To be forever without one's mother is a terribly and persistently sad experience. This is why Bessie Griffin sang "Sometimes I feel like a motherless child / a long ways from home." She wasn't just talking about mothers. She was talking about homes. The loss of home, the loss of family. The loss of a place where you belong. She was talking about African people kidnapped to America. This is why it's a Negro spiritual. To be like a motherless child a long ways from home is maybe the blackest of all black experiences.

Maybe for people like Tunde and me—the black freaks, black skaters, black rockers and black punks, the black four-track masters and black noise-rock makers—the weird social exile we were experiencing all of our lives didn't make us as unique as we thought.

Maybe, instead, it was the very thing that made us belong.

How have you handled being one of the only black dudes with your set of cultural ideas in the world where you work?

It's not that I don't think about it, but I very rarely see myself as apart from whatever crowd, or black people. Being black is something—I don't wanna say *mysterious*—but it's like, I experience interactions that make me realize that it's sort of an issue. Like, this weird bump that has to be walked around. Just in terms of meeting people and having them say some shit in front of you. It's like, I don't know where you're from or where that flies—but part of me is like, do I say something to you? Or do I just let you go into the world and wait for someone who's gonna break your neck to do it?

When I first met you that was one of the things I wondered—if your experience growing up was being one of the only black kids around white people.

Definitely when we moved to America. I lived in Nigeria for a long while, so that was not the case at all [*laughs*]. Yeah, we'd judge each other by character, weird things like that!

So backwards in Africa [*laughs*].

But, yeah, we moved back to America. I grew up in Pittsburgh.

I didn't know that! So did I, McKeesport.

Oh really?! I grew up in Hampton Township.

Oh, I had no idea. I moved away from there when I was thirteen.

Yeah, I took off when I was eighteen. It was kind of a … you wanted to leave, right?

Absolutely. I was very happy to get to New York and be like, "Ohhhh. Now I can breathe a little easy."

It's very weird—my dad brought me [to New York City] and he basically just looked at me and was like, you know what I expect from you, you know what I don't. He got

back in the car and left, no orientation, none of that shit.

Maybe that's a thing, because my dad did a very similar thing.

I'm, like, fucked. "Guess I'm going to the park! Maybe I can find some weed!"

When I think of kids like us, I think we always had the feeling we were gonna make art, but we didn't think anyone was gonna like it. We were just gonna do it anyway.

It's still kind of baffling to me. All of those *OK Calculator* things, they were just an extension of sketchbooks—very solitary work—where you're kind of processing the world around you. I was in a community of punks and indie kids, people making their own shit and not caring that much, processing the world in a very light way. That spirit of just cobbling shit together and seeing if it sounds right, that's what's carried through in the band. Especially with Dave and I. We started off painting together. I definitely never had the intention of like, "I wanna be a fucking rock star! This is what's gonna do it, I'm gonna have leather pants and frills," and all that shit. This whole stupid idea of making art, you're just like, "I don't know what else to do with myself." The world doesn't really make that much sense to me, so I don't owe it making sense.

There was a bit of a mini-movement coming out of Williamsburg at that time and you guys are kind of like the last men standing. Is that a surprise to you?

I mean, I don't keep track. It's been crazy to me that we've had this, what turned into a job, for as long as we have. The best bands break up after four or five years. Like five, tops.

Obviously your music has changed over however long it's been, sixteen, fifteen, twenty years …

Thirteen [*laughs*]. Twenty's a little …

I really wanted to say twenty for some reason, it's such a grown-up number.

It's a little too grown-up for me!

And here we are, we're old-ass men. I embrace this, I have two kids, I'm fully like, *Yeah, I'm an old man.* I'm down with it. How has aging changed *you* as an artist?

Growing up is hopefully a process of shaving off bullshit, and saying *this* is productive for the life I wanna live, and *this* is completely counterproductive to that. As a band, we've learned to shave off whatever real-life personal bullshit, individual tendencies. ... That stuff is completely over. You know what's important about your friendship, and you know what's unimportant. You know what needs to stick and what doesn't. But just as an artist, it's sort of weird. I don't feel like I've changed that much as an artist, but I feel like the time I have to devote to certain other things—spending all of my time making music has made me wanna do those things more.

You guys lost a member [bassist Gerard Smith, in April 2011]. In the movies when someone dies, everyone realizes the value of life and starts to *carpe diem* a lot. Was that your experience?

Well, my experience is anytime you have a reminder like that, nothing is promised to anyone. I guess, *carpe diem*, but if you're already *carpe diem*-ing, you just ... My whole job is jumping off a cliff and seeing what the fuck happens. When somebody that close to you passes away, instantly I'm thinking, "What does this person expect of me? Now that we're not carrying the baton together, what does this person expect of me, and how much do I want to keep to that?" And your idea of what people who have really influenced you as artists, what they'll hold you to, is pretty intense. I don't let just anybody in to make stuff with me. I feel like one of the reasons I've never been able to see the band as other than something I'm doing with my friends, or thought it was anything I could take advantage of, was because I didn't really wanna be a musician. You knew me in school, I wasn't ...

I thought of you as the animator.

Yeah, that's what I was doing. Do you know how solitary I was at that age? You try something else for a second, and then thirteen years later you're just like, "Oh, I guess I know how to do that." But while all that was happening, I was getting kind of ... blindsided by life events, so it all seemed really—it didn't seem really important.

What kind of events?

Well, my father died in 2005, while we were on tour. And my brother then died in 2008, very, very randomly. And then before that, two days before my brother died, one of my closest friends who I actually made music with at NYU committed suicide. I'm glad that I had the band to kind of occupy that time that could've been spent doing something regrettable. I might not have ended up here talking to you right now. Every time somebody leaves like that, it's kind of like the Buddhist koan of "the problem with human beings is they think they have all the time in the world." It's true—if you're not living in whatever moment you can snatch, then it's really a lot of chaos.

My mother died in 2008 of lung cancer. And the grief thing was so unwieldy, I did not expect it, I did not know how to comprehend grief in the way it unfolded. What was your way of dealing with grief, and how did it impact your ability to write?

When my father passed ... I actually don't remember much of that time, which is very odd. He was buried in Nigeria, so I remember going there for the first time in ten years, and being near my relatives, and kind of being not in New York—in somewhere super familiar, but definitely ... not New York. So I remember that. And just making sure you hold it together for other people, 'cause everyone's holding it together, and after the physical act of laying someone to rest, or beginning the acceptance period, you necessarily have to keep going. Williamsburg, like everybody at the time, I ended up drinking too much, or doing other shit that ... 2005, oh, yeah, that definitely fueled into *Cookie Mountain.* That was ... it wasn't *entirely* unpleasant, [but] it wasn't a pleasant period of time. We did all the wrong things, we did all the wrong things in the studio. And I guess that was part of it. Not going off the rails, but not really caring. You go through a period of time of not really caring what happens to you, you're just like, oh, I'm not afraid of anything. Because what else could happen to me at this point?

Growing up
is hopefully
a process of
shaving off
bullshit.

Did you feel isolated during that time?

Not really. No, that was the other thing about that time. Your community is this weird group of artists and weirdos, also a lot of friends who have your back. And that was one of the times that I realized, you know, you have a lot of acquaintances when you're running around, you have, like, two or three people that you think are close friends. But then something like *that* happens, and you realize, oh, I'm really tight with this person, this person is there for me. There's a lot of self-imposed isolation, and I'm totally fine with that. I've never been worried about being alone.

And what about when you lost a band member? I mean, that's …

Beyond band member, close friend, close enough to be your brother, and … it's a strange thing to try to put into words. Because, again, the shock of it. I never thought that this would happen. I never looked at anyone and was like, "In two years, that's it for you. You're out." I feel like that was a huge part of all of the bullshit being shaved off of the band. It was sort of like, that's a limb. It was a limb of this body of a group of friends. Primarily, that's it. And we happen to make music together, and it happens to be our job, you know, thankfully. You gotta take stock of why we're all together in that capacity.

Music is always a response to what's happening socially, politically—on some level. And you started making music after 9/11, and I think there was a certain feel, particularly in New York at that time, a little bit of nihilism, maybe just a little, "throw it all in there, it doesn't even fucking matter." And now we're at an interesting point with the economy, race in America.

I was just thinking about it yesterday. 9/11—you saw it happen on TV. And while that was happening, that was the story. *You had no idea what else was happening in the world*. It was just this, the world's eyes are here. But now, it's just like, we have a bird's-eye view of how terrible the world is. You know? And it's wonderful in a lot of ways, too, but it's also waking up and going onto Facebook and realizing, "Oh, there've been eight churches on fire—black churches—in maybe as many days," and that's

not front-page news. It's a sidebar. And what *is* front page news can be equally horrible, and just kind of realizing what's happening all over the world, I don't understand how you—and I don't think this is what you're asking—but how you encapsulate that in a song? Or in music. It's like, you can write "We Didn't Start the Fire," but it seems a little bit inefficient today [*laughs*]. There's gonna be a lot more verses.

It's almost, to me, a false separation between "This is art" and "This is political." There's a period of time when you're just like, "I'm gonna make art," but then we look out and shit has gone bonkers with race in America. It's always been, but it's definitely a theme now.

It's back, and it's better than ever [*laughs*].

Yeah, the sequel. And I wonder how you feel, do you feel like that changes what you have to do as a maker of stuff in the public discourse? And if so, how?

It's really a lot to process. It's very emotional. It's strange because it makes the act of music making or art making for me seem extremely frivolous, and then I have to ask myself why that is, and come to a conclusion about why I think that is, and it's like, *Well, what else am I gonna do?* My main faculty in life, strangely enough, is having shit fed into the back of my head and having it come out the front of my head, in some shape or form, that puts it in place. And it helps you comprehend it and hopefully very quickly lays the groundwork for you to communicate that to other people, and see why it's valuable to communicate that to other people. I personally have not figured that out yet. But I think about it a lot. And it's gotta turn into something.

Are you a Nina Simone fan at all?

Yeah.

Nina Simone is the nearest example of "I'm super political, and my politics are inseparable from what we make in the studio." Do you think that's possible for that to happen now?

I actually don't know. I don't know what it's gonna take for everyone to suddenly be like, "This person is speaking the truth about our times." You have to think about the purpose of either a protest song or a political song—protest, of course. You're decrying an injustice, maybe urging people to action. But a lot of that is preaching to the choir. I think about that a lot. If there was a way to get to people who didn't value every life—if there were some way to *really* get to them, it'd be amazing. It'd be an amazing feat. Like, if a skinhead suddenly hears a song and is like, "Shit! You know what? They're totally right! *And* I can dance to it?" You know?

I think about this a lot as a writer, like, who do I write for? I'm writing for people that generally agree, then what do I have to say to them? What do I have to tell them that is different than, "Hey, black people are humans, I know you don't know that." I don't know if this is true, but I have the impression that TV on the Radio communicates with *mostly* a white audience. Demographically speaking.

Yeah, I'd definitely say so.

And I wonder if you feel like that's different. If you look back to the sixties, Nina Simone is generally communicating with black audiences, all those artists are part of a black community. TV on the Radio's doing something different. I wonder if you feel like that's an opportunity, or if that changes the way that you talk about race in your work.

I don't think it does change it, because it's discussions we're having with each other, which yield a song. But yeah, I feel like a lot of the songs, whoever can listen to them. ... But then a song like "Wrong Way," that Kyp wrote, one of the points is about black entertainers cooning it up. The surface of rap music at a certain time was not a very productive thing for black people—this kind of like, demeaning women, excess—it turned into this form that didn't reflect the attitudes of a *lot* of people who came from those communities. If you're not doing that great, and you see those guys, you're like, "I am *really* a piece of shit. I have to do whatever I can to get to that." I don't know if that's just my twisted way of thinking about it. But yeah, I've wondered what part of a black experi-

ence is being transmitted through what I'm making. And aside from it being created by a black person ... I don't think that I've done that, you know what I mean? And not that I've strayed away from it, I just don't think I've done it.

Is that something you feel like you want to do more of?

Of course, yeah. I'm going to Nigeria in November, to see relatives. I want to reconnect with that, experience the culture. It's not even going there with a deliberate intention, but just to kind of be with people the same way I am with people here. I want to be able to go into communities that I don't live in and experience what, not what kids are like, but be there, and feel like I'm in a place where I'm doing something productive. Trying to connect, or connecting in that way through making something. It's definitely a concern, you know?

Has that increased in recent years, that sense of, *This is a concern and I need to figure something out?*

As you get older, you realize you still have the question, and then you're just like ... *fuck.* The outside world, it becomes so obvious to you—you just see what's actually happening.

It reminds me of the Ralph Ellison quote, "Black is, black ain't," from the *Invisible Man.* Blackness both exists and it doesn't exist. It's this social construct and also it's a social construct that's *real* because we're living it. Someone once said to me, "You're not a black person, you're a person having a black experience," and I have this theory that the longer you live, the blacker you become, because you have had more black experiences.

Of course, and you recognize them as such. Where before you're like, "Oh man, everyone in this room is a dickhead [*laughs*]. Oh, wait a minute, everyone is a dickhead towards me *because of me*."

Do you think you'll be making music until the wheels fall off?

No, no, no. It will be in the garage way before the wheels

No matter what you're feeling, the sun always looks so hopeful and sad in the late California afternoon.

CARVELL WALLACE

I feel more a part of the world now. Maybe that's getting older.

fall off [*laughs*]. I am definitely ready to do a lot less music. With TV on the Radio, we'll make whatever we make next and it will be fun. But I really do feel like I've got to take a break for a long time. Kendrick Lamar, he's hugely important to me, and to music and culture right now. He's achieved making pop music that is hugely important as far as message, hugely important as far as the black experience.

Musically, he's just …

Like insane, insane. Everyone is going to listen to it, but I don't know how many people are going to hang out in the room. I'm sure there are white people that completely get that record. I would assume that they're not in the majority. In my eyes he really did it, but for me the best ways that I can communicate those experiences are to make films or art. Music, for me, I can't. I would not want to make something that is attempting to do that. Musically, as far as melodies and lyrics go for me, I'm floating around in space, like, "I don't know what the fuck this is, but I'm going to look into it." I'm exploring things in a subconscious manner, not exactly trying to make it universal, but also not wanting to make it too specific either. I don't want to make songs so nailed down that someone can't get into it if they hear it.

What I hear you saying is a little bit about the difference between "I have this thing inside me I want to get it out, look, I made this thing," and "I want to give something to someone else and I want them to be encouraged and inspired by it." Because of who Kendrick is and where he came from, he is able to speak to this large group of people, particularly with music. From what you're saying, it sounds like you feel like that's more so something you can do with film.

I just feel like I can pull it off because I'm more interested in it. I've continued to make art and make films during all of this. I've made a lot of videos for the band. In a lot of ways I feel like you learn a set of tools and then you apply those tools to what you really want to do, but it's kind of like those two things coincide where you've got to turn an observation into an obligation. When you spot a void in the world and you're thinking, "How come I've never seen this before," if you keep thinking about why you've never seen it, you at least owe it to yourself to just try to fill it in. I don't see many cartoons for young black girls, so what if I made this TV show or comic or something where the hero is a ten-year-old black girl who happens to not just be a superheroine, but something way cooler than that—a little more down-to-earth? It's hugely important for someone to see themselves in the media they're being fed at that age. I'm doing something like that now and I want to turn it into a film.

That sounds optimistic.

I feel more a part of the world now. Maybe that's getting older. It's the feeling of wanting to go deeper into places I haven't been before, to challenge yourself as a human being, to be a part of something. What choice do you have? ✍

CARVELL WALLACE *is a writer, father, tech founder, and professional at being the only black guy in the room. He writes about race, music, film, love, freedom, melancholy, and ennui.*

The City Is Quiet, Too Cold to Walk Alone

Queer Presentation in Soft Cell, Jimmy Somerville, and Pet Shop Boys

1981–1986

BY ALFRED SOTO

MARC ALMOND OF SOFT CELL, 1985

I

For gay men in England, the dawn of the eighties was a time to fuck and get fucked—by each other, by AIDS, and by Margaret Thatcher's government. The young gay artists who emerged to create the pop soundtrack of this era were making new electronic sounds but were still besotted by disco's possibilities: the promise of communal release on the dance floor and the way it allowed greater liberty for self-presentation. The success of the Village People and Sylvester taught them that a mass audience will ignore a performer's sexuality if the beats are good enough.

Soft Cell, Jimmy Somerville, and Pet Shop Boys are queer acts whose singles actively redefined hetero notions of queer decadence: it could look as threatening as a sex dwarf or as banal as dogs in suburbia. Among this cadre of gay synth acts, Soft Cell were the least interested in mirroring contemporary culture, instead looking to soul music and the smuttier parts of William Burroughs's canon for inspiration. Pet Shop Boys, who first went global with "West End Girls" in 1985, put across their private obsessions—money, shopping, Chihuahuas—as communal longings set to rococo beats. Jimmy Somerville, the singer-songwriter behind Bronski Beat and the Communards, attenuated his outspoken leftism with songs that courted sentimentality.

II

Before Wikipedia, few knew that the most transgressive act of Marc Almond's career was smearing himself with cat food on stage. The runner-up: releasing a demo of Gloria Jones's "Tainted Love" as a pop single. With synths blipping like sonars and hotel-bar organs distorted into parodies of themselves, it topped the British chart when it was released in 1981, and then for a record thirteen consecutive years held steady on the *Billboard* Hot 100. It's a hit beyond a hit; the song has retained omnipresence for decades.

Central to its success was Almond's vocal. Thin, bearing an uncertain relationship to pitch, couched with his faint lisp, "Tainted Love" insinuated darker pleasures; the audience didn't need to know what Almond meant by "tainted," as he already sounded ravaged, a boy who confessed he gave his lover all he could. Soft Cell threw back to the nightclub acts of the sixties, to Weimar Germany cabaret—to a time when a performer could signal sexuality and expect the audience to get it. Soft Cell's modern look complemented Almond's trash-can Sinatra routine: berets, questionable mustaches, sleeveless leather. Appearing on *Top of the Pops*, the duo brought sex-club chic into proper English living rooms.

Their 1981 debut, *Non-Stop Erotic Cabaret,* presents ten tales of the city in which a bored young man shops for kicks, does some foul shit, gets his heart stomped, and learns how to construct a hard camp facade. The audience loved it—Soft Cell scored two more consecutive British top fives with "Bedsitter" and "Say Hello, Wave Goodbye," and cracked the American Top 40 the following year.

In *States of Desire: Travels in Gay America*, written a couple of years before the release of *Non-Stop Erotic Cabaret*, famed queer author Edmund White remarked that "no one will defend a place devoted to desire once the desire has been sated." Marc Almond tries to own that space in "Say Hello, Wave Goodbye," the album's stab at an original torch song. It's Soft Cell at its droll, moving best, with bandmate David Ball accompanying Almond's Scarlet Pimpernel vocal plumage with sampled car-horn bleats. The song rubs its artificiality in the audience's face, forcing them to accept that camp can move and astonish; it assumes we're adult enough to understand that love provokes complicated reactions. "You and me / we happen to be the standing joke of the year," Almond sings, unable to restrain the snickers. It works, though—the idea that someone in this world exists for us is worth a laugh.

The jokes kept coming but the hits stopped, and so did Soft Cell's inspiration. 1983's prophetically titled *The Art of Falling Apart* had the sick kicks, but no hooks. "Loving You, Hating Me" is a lugubrious rewrite of "Say Hello, Wave Goodbye," a parody of a pastiche. Only "Numbers" resonates, a chilling depiction of promiscuity set to a beat that squelches like body fluids in a vial. "Throw them away like Kleenex," Almond warbles.

That same year, AIDS casualties began to amass. Everything would change.

III

"This was a time when you'd be standing on the tube platform wondering which group of skinheads was going to throw you on the tracks that night," Jimmy Somerville reminisced in an interview with the *Guardian* in 2014, thirty years after the release of "Smalltown Boy." With his shorn head, jeans, and not an earring or splash of paint, the five-foot-four Somerville practiced a sartorial asceticism that was a reproof to the times—or, perhaps more precisely, to Marc Almond. A defense strategy intended to confuse or deflect those menacing skinheads? Possibly. Paired with the video for "Smalltown Boy," his self-presentation complemented the single's extravagance. It calls to mind a neighborhood tough guy covering disco-drag-performer Sylvester at the high school talent show—and *selling* it.

That last allusion matters. Like that other just-folks singer, Bernard Sumner of New Order, Somerville was a punk who loved disco. His high-pitched, keening falsetto emulated the impossible, impenetrable firmness of Donna Summer's. He used masculine pronouns. He danced badly. The expression of his sexuality was a statement. Never one to eschew political responsibilities, he was a member of the Red Wedge (a musical collective committed to the Labour Party's socialist wing) and was infuriated by the senescence of the Thatcher years: homosexual men were dying while establishment snobs like novelist Kingsley Amis penned moist valentines to the Iron Lady. For gay teens confused by the gooped-up quasi-effeminacy of Thompson Twins and Howard Jones on MTV, Bronski Beat's debut *The Age of Consent* presented itself as agitprop; its sleeve even listed the countries in and ages at which they could enjoy consensual sex. Increasingly atomized homosexual youth could dance to it, drawing on the communitarian spirit of the album's grooves.

The centerpiece is, of course, "Smalltown Boy." Praised by critic John Gill as the gay "She's Leaving Home," it is the story of a kid who realizes he'll never get the answers he wants from his parents, set to a mournful electronic throb. The song sailed into the English top five in the summer of 1984 and established itself stateside through heavy MTV airplay. Somerville's countertenor harnessed the beat yet floated above it, as if it already had set its sights elsewhere. Months earlier the Smiths had released "Hand in Glove," a landmark of ambivalent sexuality whose coded speech was folded into traditional guitar churn. "Smalltown Boy" mouthed a not-at-all-tender *fuck that* to codes.

The rest of *The Age of Consent* has trouble distinguishing the sweet from the bitter. In his music, Somerville wants it both ways. The album's only nod to the pre-Stonewall days, a cover of "It Ain't Necessarily So," recasts George Gershwin's chestnut as a bittersweet apologia, as if Somerville is backing away from the power of "Smalltown Boy." To set undistinguished romantic banalities to swooping vocal melodies in 1984 played like a rearguard action. Only once more did he write a song commensurate with his rage. The second single, "Why?," is Italo-disco fodderstompf, with spangled DX-7 synth lines and an unhinged Somerville yelling the title over and over—a rebel yell across decades of pain and abuse, beyond pathos. But "No More War," graced by a sampled horn, laments an immutable fact; he might as well have said the hell with it and sang "War, war, stupid," like Boy George's Culture Club would do several months later.

Somerville and Marc Almond traveled in the same circles, so collaboration was inevitable. Somerville and Almond advance a counternarrative (*Disco is still here, gays!*) with a medley of Donna Summer's "Love to Love You, Baby" and "I Feel Love" in 1985. The result is essentially karaoke night at the pub. Maybe that's the point—two homosexual men can have as appalling fucking taste as Dad and his mates. Almond's limitations as a singer don't save him; competing with Summer's empyrean-scraping vocals is as hopeless as an Englishman expecting a tan instead of a burn. He wobbles and warbles, looking for pitch, any pitch. Somerville does better, but we expect him to. A more subversive enterprise would've been to cover .38 Special.

The Bronski concept exhausted, Somerville and keyboardist Richard Coles recorded music that wasn't much different as the Communards but already showed signs of revolting smoothness. It's not their fault that their blunt talk dovetailed with the first half of the decade's spiky, awkward, and primitive sequencing technology. By 1986, MIDI programming had sanded down Somerville's quirks, or maybe Coles wasn't as resourceful a composer as Bronski's Larry Steinbachek and Steve Bronski. Either way, the Communards never lived up to their namesakes, the would-be revolutionaries who forced an emperor's abdication and turned France into the briefest of social-

NEIL TENNANT, 1983

JIMMY SOMERVILLE, 1984

ist republics in 1871. Their subversion emerged in driblets, and the beats muttered their faint agreement.

Still, the Communards were bigger in the UK than Bronski Beat, and even made faint American inroads. Acknowledging the collapse of their inspiration, they recorded a hi-NRG cover of disco great Thelma Houston's "Don't Leave Me This Way." It was the easiest shit to get away with in 1986, the most dance-happy year of the decade since 1981: true subversion would have been to shove this song onto BBC Radio One three years earlier. That said, the song hit big. It became the best-selling single of the year in the UK and grazed the American Top Forty. Cumulative goodwill toward Somerville helped, excusing an arrangement that sounds at least half a measure too slow and a rhythm as pneumatic as a drill press. "Don't Leave This Way" hurts the ears; it is fake enthusiasm, a smile to fool the public, a stab at assimilation that codes as resignation. Treated for years with the contempt now reserved for AIDS victims, disco returned as nostalgic aerobics. Revanchists hated disco because its submission to pleasure threatened post-sixties rock's obsession with narrative and confession; now it was okay to dance again because Reagan and Thatcher's policies said so. "Don't Leave Me This Way" fit those expectations.

As the AIDS death toll mounted in the late eighties, it wasn't enough to cover a disco chestnut: Somerville had to remind a straight majority embracing a previous generation's rebarbative political solutions that "there's more to love than boy meets girl." That phrase, the title of the last successful Communards single, rides a chugging beat heavy on synthetic bass burbles and a faint air of resignation. It's a tepid stab at trouncing Stock-Aitken-Waterman, the pop songwriting collective that owned the British charts through Thatcher's third term. "I saw your face, it caught the light, infatuation swirls inside," Somerville coos, a declaration, not a deliverance. On its release the single's title got shortened to "There's More to Love"—a final insult.

IV

After marinating in hits like "What Have I Done to Deserve This?" for years, the Pet Shop Boys released a debut that

is strikingly austere, especially compared to Bronski Beat and Soft Cell. *Please* documents the lives of men just out of their twenties whose socializing can't hope to match their fantasies, and who are burdened by that gulf—it's what distinguishes PSB from Soft Cell and Somerville. For Neil Tennant and Chris Lowe, love comes quickly, but action takes time. The synth-pop duo that recorded *Please* and those early singles yearned for lovers to match the elaborate self-construction in "Opportunities (Let's Make Lots of Money)" and "West End Girls." Call it a response to AIDS. Call it their natural discretion. "This anticipation is a stimulation," Tennant sings breathlessly on "I Want a Lover"—it's probably better stimulation than actually hooking up.

Crazy about consumer culture, Pet Shop Boys were uniquely qualified to indict it, and not without stuffing their pockets first. Early critics got them wrong: it's easier for a liberal to accept a Devastating Satire about Thatcher's England than a straightforward appeal to a lover who doctored in mathematics, studied at the Sorbonne, summers in Lake Geneva, and got bored with *To the Finland Station*. The way Pet Shop Boys regard love as commerce—as a transactional arrangement—distinguishes them from their synth-pop colleagues. Like Marc Almond, Tennant was qualified to write about pain, but where Almond sang as if he were feeling or had felt it, Tennant wrote about wanting to enter relationships in which he *might* feel pain. The question posed in "West End Girls"—"Which would you choose: a hard or soft option?"—isn't one that the Neil Tennant of 1986 would answer. He got off on presenting the dilemma.

It's odd to call any Pet Shop Boys album underrated, but *Please* enters most discussions simply as the home of their only American No. 1 single. On *Please*, Tennant is tentative and rather gauche, like the beats. It's the old story: the young man hitting the town with last night's paycheck in his wallet. Everyone looks beautiful, and he gratifies his writerly instincts by making wry observations about East End boys and West End girls over Tanqueray and tonics. He craves distance because it's not only the English thing to do, it's the stance that makes him most attractive to those beautiful strangers he's eyeing. Critics often use "irony" and "sarcasm" interchangeably; in a PSB performance, irony meant the disjunction between how they present things versus how they are to the rest of us. The songs aren't sarcastic in the usual sense:

"Tainted Love" insinuated
darker pleasures; he
already sounded ravaged,
a boy who confessed he
gave his lover all he could.

"Why?" is a rebel
yell across decades
of pain and abuse,
beyond pathos.

Tennant's characters really want to be as superficial as they claim.

Yet the anodyne quality of much of *Please* veils unspoken hurts; the subtexts were a code for anyone who wanted to peer beneath the glitz. On "Love Comes Quickly," producer Stephen Hague double-tracks Tennant into submission, the rhythm as unrelenting as a beating heart on a dance floor—and we all know how great and awful a crush is when the beloved's dancing a few inches away, oblivious. Sampled trombones and a ticky-tick rhythm mirror the singer's impatience in "I Want a Lover." Purportedly a song about the thrill of picking up a guy, it sounds like a fantasy; when Lowe follows "Driving through the night is so *exciting*" with a sampled car crash, Tennant sounds like the crash made him hornier than the guy did.

Album closer "Why Don't We Live Together" sums up *Please* better than the singles. Probably the Boys' greatest should-have-been-a-hit, it examines themes rarely explored in pop music: compromise, accommodation, settling. Tennant has never been more accessible than when he admits, "You may not always love me / I may not care." The key word is *may*, as devastating a qualifier as the caesura in "I love you, you pay my rent" on a later and even greater hit song. He sounds *giddy*, turned on by his own honesty. As Lowe goes bonkers on the arrangement, piling up bass stutters and burps, synth-harmonica solos and thick coats of drums, and Tennant bursts into falsetto because, *well, why not*, adulthood sounds as exciting as adolescence.

V

By 1987 the commercial retreat for Somerville and Almond had begun—slowly in Somerville's case and terminally in Almond's. Neil Tennant and Chris Lowe, however, were only beginning to make lots of money. Three more UK No. 1 singles followed "West End Girls," and four more top tens in America before the end of what critic Tom Ewing coined their "imperial phase," when everything they touched turned gold. Through Madchester, Britpop, and boy bands, Pet Shop Boys' commercial propulsion

never sputtered. To speculate how Tennant and Lowe shaped their public selves by noting Almond and Somerville's efforts isn't farfetched. Because Soft Cell and Bronski Beat reached their artistic peaks before *Please*, it's hard to resist the temptation to regard them as cautionary tales. Surely Tennant, a pop journalist before he stepped into a recording studio, followed the arcs of their careers.

As the AIDS crisis worsened, the age demanded social protest and aesthetic specificity. To ask "why" as Jimmy Somerville did in 1984 was easier than explaining how gay men meet a friend for a pint, walk their dogs, shop for groceries—the boring stuff of living. Positing gay men at the height of AIDS as *just men* would've been genuinely transgressive. Which is why Marc Almond's dilemma looks poignant in retrospect. Soft Cell's material got more absurd as Ball's creative well dried. Settling into cult status as a solo artist, Almond at last found the appropriate settings for his pulp, telling these stories with a sigh.

Meanwhile Pet Shop Boys told stories, period. Their characters figuring themselves out as sexual beings led to a confusion that is satisfying aesthetically and honest as a mode of being. By 1988, they could acknowledge their objects of lust but keep a safe distance in case the audience freaked out (and in the United States, they might have). In the video for "Domino Dancing," Tennant and Lowe align their vision with the aloof female character for whose sake a pair of Puerto Rican twinks are willing to wrestle in the sea. They understood that the mostly heterosexual mass audience wanted mixed signals from their pop stars. The ambiguity—together with the suppleness with which their songs reflected the public's attitudes toward their faith, their money, their lusts—gave more observant fans a frisson of pleasure; they could take pride in receiving the signals while singing along to another brilliant chorus. PSB made it okay to accept surface, to rejoice in it, to allow it to reflect the gruesome, swollen truth of their straight chartmates.

ALFRED SOTO *is a student media coordinator and instructor of journalism at Florida International University. He is an editor at the* Singles Jukebox. *Previously, he was features editor at* Stylus Magazine. *His work has appeared in the* Village Voice, Billboard, Slate, Spin, *and* Red Bull Music Academy, *among others. He lives in Miami.*

Beginning to See the Light

History is written with hope, a prayer, and by a very, very good community of archivists.

BY HALEY MLOTEK

ILLUSTRATIONS BY AMY BLUE

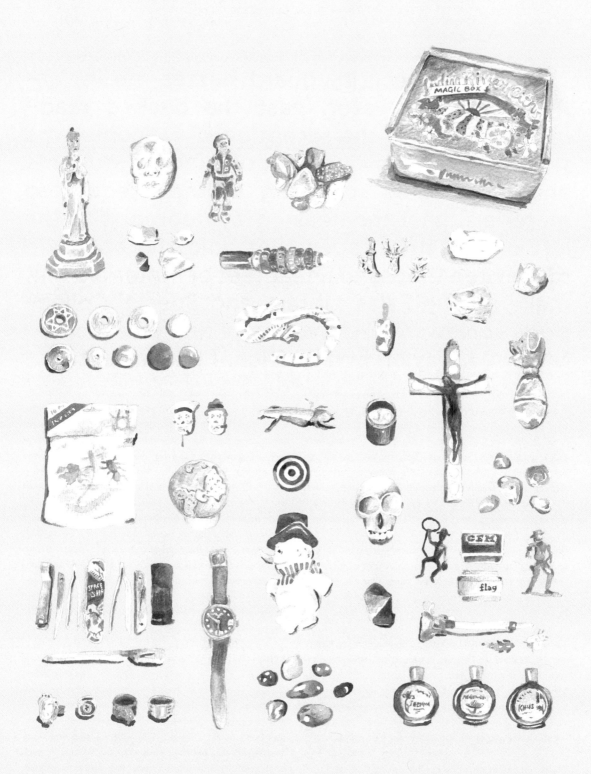

After the security guard buzzes me in, after the elevator, past the hushed reading room where the receptionist welcomes me with a silent wave in a room full of students and researchers squinting at their requested materials, past the heavy gray door, just to the left of the steel cages that hold the approximately ten thousand linear feet of materials that make up the Fales Library and Special Collections at New York University, I find the director, Marvin J. Taylor, in his office. I take a seat.

He offers to tell me about his favorite use of enjambment in popular music. *"I guess I should've known,"* he says, or chants, keeping time with one palm lightly slapping his forearm, *"by the way you parked your car / sideways / that it wouldn't last."* He pauses for a moment so we can both experience the pleasure of that syntax, that rhythm. "I mean, that is enjambment beyond enjambment. I use it if I'm teaching the concept. It's a really brilliant structure, and that appeals to me."

I've never heard the word *enjambment*—the continuation of a sentence, without pauses, beyond the end of a line—before this moment. But I know every word to Prince's "Little Red Corvette." I understand what Taylor is trying to tell me.

Taylor is part of a small but vital group of archivists, librarians, booksellers, and private collectors compiling physical records of a not-so-distant past. Together and separately, their collections contain objects of undisputed importance by artists everyone knows; they also retain collections of objects full of unknowns, items saved without context by artists whose names are spoken by only a chosen few.

Music is the ultimate form of ephemera in art. A song is an artifact with no one true physical form, no possible way of being seen, held, or felt, and because it is subject to the ever-changing whims of technology, songs can too easily slip away before being safely preserved for future generations. A musical genre, such as punk or hip-hop, struggles to be contained and contextualized as its influence remains ongoing. That's when donors and collectors look at everything that circles a song, like the flyers for a show, the T-shirts sold by a band, the recordings of notable performances. These are the artifacts that can explain, or at least attempt to define, a feeling specific to a time that has long since passed; these are the artifacts that can be pointed to as a kind of shortcut for instant understanding. And there's a large amount of that kind of collection to be found, particularly if you are measuring in linear feet. The institutionalized preservation of music—in universities, libraries, and museums—is where artists and collectors alike can find solace and security. Here, they can trust that their work of any medium is held only in the safest hands.

At the Fales Library, the "ten thousand linear feet" metric is a directional guide: that is the length of every single item if it were laid out in an unbroken line of the approximately one hundred thousand media elements. The steel cages that comprise the different collections (as of this writing, that includes Downtown, Nightclubbing, and Riot Grrrl, among others) hold their precious cargo in boxes, each item carefully sealed in its necessary protective shield, like Mylar sheets. Framed prints of Kathy Acker's book covers hang in front of the rows of boxes, propped up on steel; behind those images are Richard Hell's journals and

correspondence safe in their own boxes. Other rows hold flyers promoting musical guests at the Palladium, one of the most popular nightclubs in New York during the late 1980s, and here you can find the materials promoting performances by Ric Ocasek, Frank Zappa, and the Mamas and the Papas, just to name a few. VHS tapes capture the grainy scenes of New York's punk scene: Divine performing with the Dead Boys at CBGB on one tape, the Voidoids on another. The Dead Kennedys and Iggy Pop appeared at Hurrah's; the Cramps were at Irving Plaza.

When Taylor arrived at NYU in 1994, none of these items were there. They were still dispersed across the city and country, held in apartments and storage units, unsure of their own value. At the time, NYU was undergoing a shift in its educational objectives. It hired Taylor to make its library a research destination for scholars from all over the world. There were, by Taylor's estimate, less than five hundred linear feet of archival materials, and most of it was fiction. "Fix it," he recalls being told. "But they weren't sure what 'it' was."

Within a year, Taylor knew how to fix that elusive "it." The resulting archive became what is now known as the Downtown Collection, the artifacts, papers, and ephemera related to the art, music, and writing produced in lower Manhattan between 1974 and 1984. Taylor suggested it for a number of practical reasons: location, for one, since the rough geographical outline of the downtown scene was quite literally in NYU's backyard. Access was another, since as a self-described "proto-punk" kid himself, Taylor knew just who to ask for donated materials. And urgency was third: Taylor feared the loss of these materials forever, since such a significant number of artists and musicians were dying or had died of AIDS.

In the beginning, Taylor personally sought out artists he believed would strengthen the collection: David Wojnarowicz, the writer, filmmaker, painter, graffiti artist, and musician who died in 1992, was one of his first big acquisitions, primarily because Taylor knew Wojnarowicz's presence in the archive would encourage his peers to also volunteer their materials. Those instincts paid off; since then, Taylor spends less time actively soliciting than receiving offers from private collectors, donors, and dealers who can trust him to properly care for their work in an academic environment. The Downtown Collection is known for its multidisciplinary approach, taking works of any and all mediums and not just the predominant mode the artist was known for. For Taylor, archives are meant to be "big and sprawling and messy and exciting," he tells me. "The really rich collections can be used for so many different things. It's not just research. People create new work; we have artists coming in and looking at [the archive] to create."

When I asked him what his donors and collectors have in common when they are so diverse in artistic scope, his answer is simple: history. They are often warding off the specter of loss, particularly for the queer artists who are no longer able to speak for themselves. "There's a sense, especially among the younger queer kids, that they've lost their history. A whole generation of uncles died ... I've been working with younger activists who want to do something about this, and we've come up with storytelling," he explains. "I think the people who come to us know there's something in their time that they have to document."

When faced with several thousand feet of history made tangible—flesh made archive, scrawled notes made sacred, all sheltered in one floor of the NYU library—I confronted a bias I think is shared with many people who don't engage with libraries or archives. When we look back on lists of names and dates, there is the tendency to see it all as inevitable: to see, with the clarity that only distance is supposed to bring, how perfectly aligned each

moment of historical significance was to the preceding or following moments. *This happened,* which meant *that happened,* which led to *this*, the sense of fated destination. "Of course," we shrug. Of course he founded that band, of course she performed that song, of course that club opened and of course that club closed.

Taylor and his archivist peers operate under a different set of assumptions: how easily this could all have *never happened,* or, worse, been lost forever. Seeing the vast rows of boxes, and then holding an item as commonplace as a poster in your hand, is a reckoning with how fragile these items are. Their decay was almost guaranteed; their status as holy existed only after a sanctuary was made for them. History, the cliché goes, is written by the winners. That's not exactly right. History is a hope, a prayer, and a very, very good community of archivists.

Lisa Darms, the senior archivist at the Fales Library and the sole curator of its Riot Grrrl collection, works in the office next to Taylor. Darms founded the Riot Grrrl collection in 2009; she grew up attending punk shows in Victoria, Canada, before attending Evergreen State College in Olympia, Washington, at the same time the riot grrrl scene was beginning. As she says in the introduction to *The Riot Grrrl Collection,* a companion volume to the archive published by the Feminist Press in 2013, she had no idea that the riot grrrl movement spanning 1989 to 1996 would become so significant to so many people in the decades following.

Like Taylor did with Wojnarowicz, Darms started with two essential members of riot grrrl: Kathleen Hanna and Johanna Fateman, knowing that with their extensive archives secured, other people would want to offer their own collections as well. Becca Albee, Tammy Rae Carland, Sheila Heti, and Mimi Thi Nguyen were just a

few of the crucial members who gave their own collections to Darms.

While Darms has a personal connection to riot grrrl, her job is to curate a space that is as comprehensive as possible, not just one that reflects her personal tastes or sensibilities. In archival terms, the collection is practically a baby at barely six years old. Yet while it accounts for less than 1 percent of the Fales Library's physical holdings, it comprises 15 percent of all requests for research. The possibilities for future work are endless: Darms collects with an eye looking beyond what exists in the present or past.

Darms points to *Gunk,* a zine by Ramdasha Bickceem, as a personally treasured piece. *Gunk* ran five issues, originally intended to be a skateboarding and music zine, but like Bickceem writes in *Gunk* no. 4, "as fate would have it, we broadened our horizons." She reviews the Riot Grrrl Convention that took place in Washington, DC, dissecting the problems plaguing both the title and practice of riot grrrl: that in their attempt to leave behind the toxicity of white masculine punk culture, its pioneers had created their own unequal and uneven landscape prioritizing one kind of white female voice above all others, and attempts to explain this to other riot grrrls amounted to "preaching to the choir."

In 2015, Gabby Bess visited this zine at the Fales Library. Bess wrote a long essay for the website Broadly.com, about both *Gunk* and Bickceem, taking what was written decades ago and putting it in the context of today's music industry. Here, the availability of *Gunk* provides a record that is both a gain and a loss: proof of what Bickceem reported, an absence of voices in a burgeoning musical moment, but used by Bess to create new work, new words, new critiques for a new time.

Darms is limited to what she can physically acquire: there

are collections she mentions across America, Canada, and Europe that she'd like to have in order to expand the scope of the Riot Grrrl collection, but the process is slow and meticulous. As the senior archivist, Darms handles every area of archival management: she teaches students, assists researchers, and works on fundraising, but her principal job is working with potential and active donors, either seeking out new collections and materials or maintaining relationships with existing donors. By the time Darms meets with them, they've already discussed what kind of materials are appropriate for Fales. "Hopefully, when you get it, it's really good, rich, unique materials, like journals, correspondence, materials they might have used in their writing or creative notebooks." Once it's at the library, they accession the materials, meaning they create a subrecord of the donation within the larger record of the collection. They'll also de-accession anything they don't need, a fancy way of saying discarding it. "Like a toothbrush or whatever," Darms offers as an example, before reconsidering. "Although sometimes we do want their toothbrush. But mostly we don't."

Later in the same introduction to *The Riot Grrrl Collection,* Darms writes that as she "studied to become an archivist in the mid-2000s at NYU, [she] realized that 'historical importance' is partially a result of what's saved and preserved by institutions." According to Darm, our ideas of what is, or what deserves, safekeeping behind lock and key is often defined more by what is available than anything else. Access infuses an object with its own kind of sacred power; a shrine to an idol, even reproduced in mimeograph or embodied by something as commonplace as a toothbrush, is still a shrine.

In July 2015, I visited the Smithsonian Institute to meet two of the curators of its soon-to-be-opened National Museum of African American History and Culture. Timothy Anne Burnside and Dwan Reece both began their careers at the Smithsonian as interns. Like Taylor, Burnside and Reece come from musical backgrounds: piano and percussion for Burnside, singing for Reece. Both agree that music needs its own place within the hallowed walls of museums. "We're a museum of history and culture," Reece tells me. "Music is a cultural product. It allows you to explore history, politics ... it's not just what you see on a manuscript or what you hear. It's the circumstances in which it was created, written, produced, where it's performed, what people do with it. It's rich with those kinds of stories." When the museum opens in fall 2016, eleven inaugural exhibitions will be on display. One of them, *Musical Crossroads*, is an examination of music beginning with the very first African people in America and continuing right up to the present. The week we met, Burnside had just returned from one of her many travels around the country collecting artifacts: a trip home from Atlanta was particularly fraught, as she tried to return with Public Enemy's iconic boombox in tow, the same one seen onstage for the band's It Takes a Nation of Millions to Hold Us Back tour and personally donated by Chuck D. She checked her bag and brought it on the plane as her carry-on. She fought TSA guards who wanted to take it apart and inspect it from the inside out. As the last person to board, she had to ask the flight attendants to rearrange all the other stowed luggage so that the boombox could remain as physically close to her as possible. The pilot came on the loudspeaker to make a joke: "Lady, where is this thing going? The Smithsonian?"

The goal of the center is one that is complementary to an archive but runs on a parallel course: here, admission requires nothing more than the purchase of a ticket, and all items are on display instead of sealed until they're needed for an express purpose like research. As an exhibition that prizes popular music—music by the people, of the people—accessibility means crystal-clear visibility for as many visitors as possible.

"I'm a champion of the underdog, and I'm a champion of the general public," Reece says when I ask her if there are any overriding themes in her own work and musical preferences. "I feel an affinity for artists that have not been well represented or well studied, and what kind of complex stories we can possibly tell with objects that belonged to them. I always think people benefit from not only knowing these stories, but also having a way to make connections between these stories."

Burnside began collecting with, in her words, a "shooting for the stars" mentality. She set her sights on J Dilla's sound equipment, particularly his Akai MPC and synthesizer, hoping to do justice to the producer who died in 2006. It took five years of conversations with Dilla's mother, Maureen Yancey, before she agreed to the Smithsonian donation. "I never tried to convince her it was something she should do if she had reservations. It was representative of her son being gone, to part with that equipment and to part with that piece of him."

The balance between the living and the dead—a museum exhibition as a wake—is a line Reece and Burnside tread very carefully. J Dilla's equipment will be accessible to many visitors, but in a way that makes painfully clear the loss of his life. This is the frequent barrier Burnside and Reece have come up against as they prepare to present their impressive catalog of contemporary objects: Burnside recalls Russell Simmons vocalizing his opposition to the donation of hip-hop-related materials to the Smithsonian, asking, "Does this mean hip-hop is over, because it's in the Smithsonian now?"

Far from being over, the National Museum of African American History and Culture aims to prevent anything of value from slipping through history's cracks. "I saw what happened with jazz," Burnside explains. "There were missed opportunities, missed chances, things were physically lost and nobody knows where they ended up. There's a battle over an estate or a flood. Things happen. I thought, Well, why can't we do this right now? Why can't we start collecting from people who are still here? Why do they have to be dead?"

In museums, presence is defined, paradoxically, by absence: the ability to see with your own eyes a piece of history is tempered by a pane of glass, a lock, a key. The object is *here,* of course, but for display purposes only: the object can be in only one place at a time, which relies on the generosity of families, friends, and owners letting go in favor of some kind of institutionalized greater good. "Loss is a major, major, theme," Burnside says of her work. "Whenever you're talking about taking things away from someone, that's loss. Whenever you're talking about preserving the legacy of someone who has passed on, that's loss. It's these moments that are equal parts celebratory and not retrospective. Reflective."

"Every time I frame a piece from my collection," Bryan Ray Turcotte, the coauthor of *Fucked Up and Photocopied,* tells me, "I usually end up smashing it out again because it feels wrong to be covered by a layer of glass. Punk behind glass just feels wrong."

Originally published in 1999 and reissued for the fifteenth anniversary in 2014, *Fucked Up and Photocopied* is a book that documents the flyers and posters of the North American punk scene between 1977 and 1985; the materials therein have been exhibited in the Los Angeles Museum of Contemporary Art.

Turcotte, whose personal collection was last counted at well over one hundred thousand individual pieces, is right that punk has never been a movement that thrived behind glass, but it is a genre that has, since its very beginning, invited close attention and interpretation from various cultural institutions. Museums, such as the Metropolitan Museum of Art, stage shows about punk fashion; prestigious publishers like Rizzoli release heavy coffee-table books celebrating the evolution of punk's aesthetics in North America and England.

The first time I read one such book—*Punk: An Aesthetic,* edited by Johan Kugelberg and Jon Savage—I came across a quotation from the artist Stewart Home that I have thought about often in the years since. "Punk rock is a receding object," he said. "As one approaches, it disappears."

The institutionalized settings of museums and universities have become the final destination approached by personal collectors like Turcotte and dealers such as Brian Cassidy, whom I visited at his appointment-only bookshop in Silver Springs, Maryland. Cassidy, like Turcotte, began a collection inspired by his own tastes, starting with the Beat poets and the writers who inspired them. Today he calls his specialty "the twentieth-century avant-garde," which includes poetry, modern art, conceptual art, Fluxus, and music with an emphasis on rock and punk. "I like to say outsiders and weirdos," he says to summarize. As examples of particularly valuable items for sale, he points to the silkscreen posters for a John Cage residency at the University of Illinois; a flyer for Joy Division's first show in Manchester after the release of *Unknown Pleasures,* designed by Jon Savage; and the original slides of Jim Morrison and Jimi Hendrix performing in New York in 1968.

Cassidy sells to a number of institutions, including Darms and Taylor, to help them round out an existing collection or archive. "Those materials help to re-create the milieu in which some of the other material occurred in or was created in." Alternatively, libraries and special collections use them for exhibitions that promote popular access to

the institutional archive, ensuring that more people are drawn to visit. Rather than disappearing, the artifacts stay constant even as they're passed through academic, exhibitionist, and consumer channels.

Turcotte mentions that his ultimate goal is to see his personal collection grow, preferably in a library rather than a museum. "A place where punks, artists, teachers, historians, and fans can come see it firsthand. Anything would be better than glass and velvet ropes," he reiterates. "I do feel that handling the collection actually preserves it better. These are not fragile and delicate items. Most of them survived being stapled to walls and telephone polls and hot sweaty pockets in someone's jeans in the pit of a punk show. They can survive the hands of people who love them."

In *The Downtown Book,* the companion volume to the collection, Lynne Tillman writes: "'I remember' is a heart-stopper ... 'I remember' is as powerful as 'I love,' a trigger, and just a subject and verb. Both capture emotions left out of histories."

Capturing an emotion left out of a history is like a song: it can't be held or touched or seen. But that is, I realized, the ultimate artifact being preserved. The Fales Collection, the Smithsonian Institute, and the private booksellers and collectors like Cassidy and Turcotte represent only a small portion of the work being done to archive other musicians and artists in America. Collections at Yale University are working to document the American punk music scene, and Harvard University and Cornell University both host their own hip-hop collections.

The patterns emerging from all of these separate places is sometimes obvious: a focus on interdisciplinary art and education, access to urban centers, a personal affinity for certain musical genres and scenes. Some patterns are less tangible. Archives require an unfailing commitment to artists who can no longer speak for themselves. They're required to tangle with the egos of the living, asking them to take something personal and make it politically public. All are tied to death; none are funerals. All of them have elements of the sacred; none are churches.

The experience of spending so much time with these collections has its own kind of holiness. Realizing that there is so much to know, and learn, and discover, is an exhilarating one. The work will never be done, each artifact a brick for a road that gets longer and longer, traveling farther away from its origins toward something we can't yet know.

At our meeting, Reece acknowledged her own limitations and the limitations of her work. "I don't know every story and I don't pretend to, but when people come to us, I look at that as a point of generosity to share these stories. I feel like we're caretakers. We have an obligation to respect these stories and champion them as well."

Because these collections exist, they're a preventative measure against loss. Their presence gives us the possibility of a collective history, one that can continue to grow in comprehensive scope and emotional connections, either to reference or to rail against. Both are useful, necessary constructs that force all participants in popular culture to question the relevance of our shared past while we occupy a shared present. We hear, see, and feel them in our memories and in the archives; we hold the work in our hands, and we measure them in feet. ✑

HALEY MLOTEK *is the editor of the* Hairpin. *She lives in New York.*

Do It All Night

The Story of Prince's *Dirty Mind*

BY MICHAELANGELO MATOS

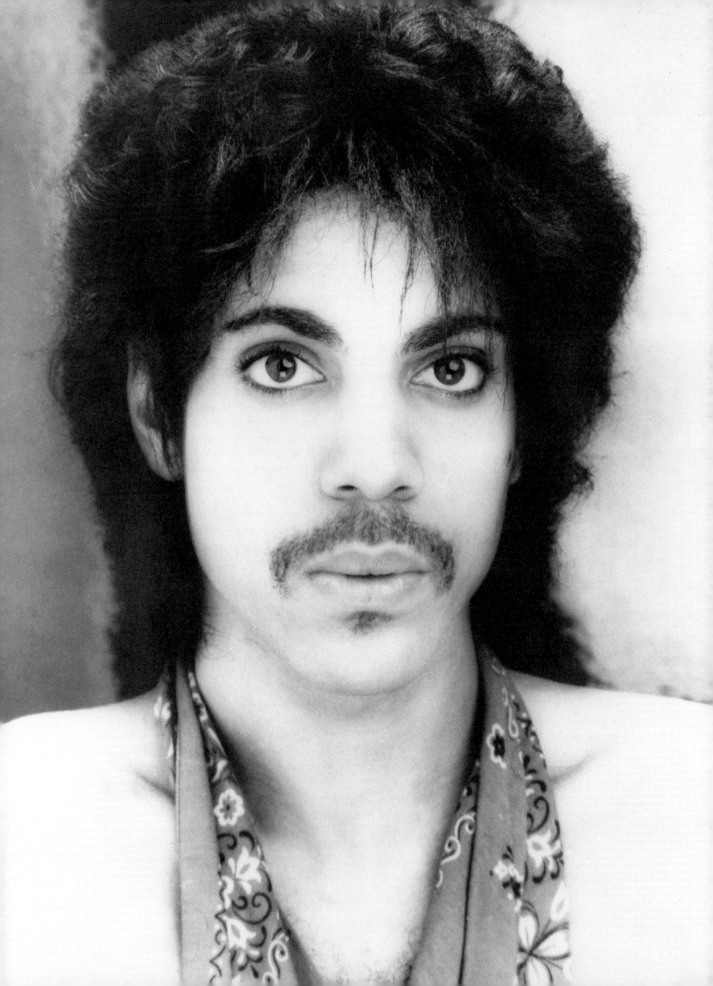

It's not entirely your fault if you don't quite understand why Prince was such a big deal in the eighties.

In the digital era, the Minneapolis auteur has made his catalog relatively inaccessible, recently removing it from mainstream streaming services in protest of their underpayment. This is principled and laudable, even as it contrasts sharply with prevailing realities. That means it's *très* Prince—done with the belief that his legacy should be regarded *his* way. In an era when reissues of reissues help to keep back catalogs alive, this is not a particularly canny management practice. But this same stubborn, altruistic insistence on doing things his way is what made Prince, at one point, the most exciting artist in the world.

When Prince signed to Warner Bros. Records in 1977 at age nineteen, his contract called not only for an unusual degree of creative control—Prince was to write, produce, and play every instrument on his recordings, à la Stevie Wonder—but also explicitly stated that he be part of the label's pop roster, not its R&B one. This distinction would shape the entirety of his career to come.

His first album, 1978's *For You*, was all falsetto, and also ambitious. His grasp was sure but the material wasn't quite there yet, though "Soft and Wet" raised a few eyebrows: Stevie may have been a twelve-year-old genius, but Prince was a teenage prodigy delivering an ode to pussy. His coy falsetto delivery and even coyer lyrics ("Your love is soft and wet") laid over tricky drumming and layered harmonies served notice: not only could the kid play and sing, he could *hear*.

A year later, everything changed. Critic Chris Herrington once called *Prince* (1979) the greatest teen-pop album ever made, and it's difficult to argue the point, though "Bambi" (in which a crazed-sounding Prince screams to a woman he wants to sleep with to renounce her lesbianism over a heavy guitar solo) is not quite high school fare. But there's so much give on it that he could have stayed in its lane forever and iced Ray Parker Jr. on his way to lunch. "I Wanna Be Your Lover" crossed him over to pop (No. 11) and led to an infamous *American Bandstand* appearance in which he fucked with host Dick Clark by refusing to speak, instead holding fingers up to indicate numbers and smirking the whole time. Prince's persona was that of the Avenging Geek—with the proviso that he would be much more capable in bed, since that was pretty much all he sang about.

For years, Prince had played with junior high and high school classmates from Minneapolis's north side. The talent pool was deep and Prince could have picked anyone. The band's roster was male, female, black, white—a mixture clearly modeled on Sly and the Family Stone. He also cranked his guitar in concert, not just on "Bambi" but on *everything*. Reviewing one of his first live outings fronting the band he'd later dub the Revolution, the *Soho Daily News* in February 1980 wrote of his show at the Bottom Line: "Judging by [his second] album, you'd never know that Prince is anything but a rock dilettante. In concert, it's clearly his lifeline."

This had been the case for some time. Not only had the young tyro bicycled to his local record store in north Minneapolis (during the sixties and seventies, where the majority of the Twin Cities' then-minuscule black population lived) to pick up new James Brown seven-inches, he'd been playing hard-rock covers in bars since he was a teenager. "I'm not saying I'm better than anybody else," he told *Rolling Stone* in 1990. "But you'll be sitting there at the Grammys, and U2 will beat you. And you say to yourself, 'Wait a minute. I can play that kind of music, too. I played La Crosse [Wisconsin] growing up, I know how to do that, you dig? But *you* will not do 'Housequake'"—a JB-indebted funk bomb from 1987's *Sign O' the Times*.

Prince's first dozen headlining club shows began at the Roxy in West Hollywood on November 26, 1979, and served as warm-ups for his real coming-out as a live performer: opening forty-two dates for Rick James's Fire It Up tour in February and March of 1980. On that tour, Prince typically stayed on script: seven songs culled from the first two albums. With one major exception the following year, this was not only the last time Prince would be anybody's opening act but one of the few times he followed a set list so exactly for an entire tour. That creative restlessness aligned him more readily with the make-it-new sensibility of sixties rock than it did eighties pop's carefully laid marketing plans.

Prince had allegedly been added to Rick James's tour to bolster the headliner's waning draw. "It was a rough period for Rick," Prince's guitarist Dez Dickerson told biographer Dave Hill. "We would go over like gangbusters, because the black audience was just dying for

something new." James himself famously loathed the Minnesota imp, telling *Rolling Stone*, "I can't believe people are gullible enough to buy Prince's jive records." James called Prince "a mentally disturbed young man. He's out to lunch. You can't take his music seriously. He sings songs about oral sex and incest." James would exact his revenge—as Prince's 1980 opening act Teena Marie told Alan Light—by allegedly stealing Prince's programmed synthesizers and using them on 1981's *Street Songs*, and then "sent them back to him with a thank-you card." Prince returned the favor when he persuaded James's date to the American Music Awards, Denise Matthews, to join Vanity 6.

Prince responded to the pressure and tedium of tour by working. Though parts of his subsequent album *Dirty Mind* came together in his basement studio, half of the album's material was composed during the Fire It Up tour. In the BBC documentary "Hunting for Prince's Vault," keyboardist Matt "Dr." Fink said that Prince wrote "When You Were Mine" on the balcony of a Florida hotel room, declining to join the rest of the band on a day trip to Walt Disney World.

Rick James had a lot to say about Prince, most of it bad. In 1983, he told *Blues & Soul*: "He doesn't want to be black. My job is to keep reality over this little science fiction creep. And if he doesn't like what I'm saying about him, he can kiss my ass. He's so far out of touch with what's really happening, it makes me angry." Prince was well acquainted with the reality of race in the record business. Crossing over from the commercial exile of R&B (a genre acutely feeling the aftereffects of disco's backlash) to rock's mainstream was vital to anyone in his situation—and most particularly as a native of lily-white Minneapolis. Writer Steve Perry quoted Jimmy Jam as saying, "Black musicians [in Minneapolis in the seventies] were going, 'We can't get a job, we better make a demo tape or something and try to get up out of here.' ... That's why we made it out here. Not that we had more talent [than the white musicians]; nothing like that. We just had more initiative, because there was nothing here for us."

That situation was writ large at the dawn of the eighties—which is to say, Prince knew precisely how fucked he'd be if he didn't stipulate that he be treated as a pop act instead of an R&B one. This was the dark ages of R&B crossover. Billboard's year-end 1981 singles list featured only eight black records in the Top 40; in 1979, there had been sixteen (and seven black records

Prince's persona was that of the Avenging Geek—with the proviso that he would be much more capable in bed, since that was pretty much all he sang about.

Prince knew precisely how fucked he'd be if he didn't stipulate that he be treated as a pop act instead of an R&B one.

in the top ten). The number had halved in two years.

"The record industry provides probably the strangest example of segregation since South African apartheid—a frequent, unspoken separation of blacks and whites that subtly and insidiously damages our industry," Prince's publicist Howard Bloom wrote in an August 1981 commentary piece for *Billboard*. "If a black act's record is rock & roll and belongs on AOR radio, that's too bad. The black special markets department drops the record because it's not appropriate to black radio. And the white AOR and pop departments generally refuse to touch the record because of the color of the artist who made it." This also worked in reverse, as Bloom pointed out: Devo's "Whip It" got little play on AOR, Devo's so-called "natural" constituency, but went gold in part because the record had broken on black radio thanks to WGPR-FM DJ the Electrifying Mojo—a black radio legend and Detroit techno forefather, as well as the first DJ to broadcast Prince's music to the Motor City.

Although Prince liked to kid new wave, he also saw its openness as a beacon of the future. In 1981 he told an interviewer, "They're ready for a change, I can sense it. Change in music, change in lifestyle. They want to be open and they want to dress any way they want to at the gigs. ... Tradition at black concerts a lot of times was to wear your best clothes, to come looking really dapper. It's not like that at our concerts. There are a lot of black kids out there, but they're like open-minded and free, and they want to have a good time." Guitarist Wendy Melvoin told *Spin* that when she joined Prince's band in 1983, "We were still seen as part of the underground. I was proud of that."

Bloom was ready to put his ideals into action, writing in a memo to Prince's then-manager Steve Fargnoli, "I'd suggest booking him two dates in each market: a date as a second act on the bill to a major black headliner like Cameo, Parliament, etc., and a date at the local new wave dance club. ... Neither date will conflict with the other." He added: "Ads in publications like the *Prairie Sun*, *Night Rocker News*, and *Oasis de Neon* are dirt cheap, and they reach a staunch record-and-ticket buying audience." The reason for all this, of course, was *Dirty Mind*, which Jean Williams—Billboard's founding R&B editor—tut-tutted over: "The front cover has Prince standing donned in an open jacket with a handkerchief around his neck and in a pair of black briefs. Maybe it's meant to be sexy. The back cover gets better (or worse). Prince is lying down with the same 'outfit,' however, this time you get a look at his legs and what is he wearing? A pair of thigh high stockings. The effect is one of a nude man dressed in a pair of thigh high stockings."

Dirty Mind was not just a rock album by a black artist but one that was sold by Warner Bros. *as an album*, rather than simply as a hit single's expansion pack. *Dirty Mind* yielded only one R&B hit ("Uptown" reached No. 5) and had no success on the pop singles charts. At that time, the album audience was considered very different from the one for singles—"serious" listeners versus casual—a difference that Warners' marketing department was particularly adept at exploiting. However, this was a distinction that was creeping toward irrelevance: within three years, the "tentpole" album, spinning off endless hit singles à la Michael Jackson's *Thriller*, would be the major-label norm. But the idea of a crossover from R&B to new wave was both viable and novel in 1980—just ask Rick James, the self-crowned "King of Punk-Funk."

Little of James's music—or Prince's, for that matter—actually resembled new wave's willful primitivism. "For a lot of black people the word 'punk' had connotations of homosexuality, and there's always that macho thing with funk," Dez Dickerson told Dave Hill. Dickerson himself "was put off by people with no intention of knowing how to play. Then after a while, the spirit and the attitude of it began to appeal to me ... I was impressed by the idea of scaling things down, and making them more simple."

Prince's new wave leanings weren't surprising considering that he was a regular attendee as well as an onstage fixture at First Avenue, the downtown Minneapolis club that regularly showcased new wave and independent artists—a former employee recalls Prince being kicked out of the club one afternoon, prior to opening hours, when he was caught *in flagrante* with a woman in the men's-room stall. But even early on, Prince was interested in making his own scene rather than joining someone else's; he'd let himself be marketed as "new wave" while simultaneously disdaining it. To wit: at the end of the first side of the Time's 1982 LP *What Time Is It?* (one of many Prince ghostwritten and ghost-produced albums from this period), the band sneers, "We don't like new wave!"

There's no mistaking "When You Were Mine" for anything but a new wave song—it has organ from the Jimmy Destri (Blondie)/Steve Nieve (Elvis Costello and the Attractions) playbook, a stiff beat, and nervous guitar. The song's urgency was built into its structure. As the late Paul Williams pointed out, the verses keep retracting: The first verse is twelve lines. The second verse is eight lines. The third verse is four lines. Each verse takes us to the chorus faster, as well as to the song's central dozen-note riff, which is both keynote and denouement. This was increasingly essential to Prince's shows, in which, as Dave Hill pointed out, "one song would jump straight into the next with little explanation from the stage—another punk technique."

If *Dirty Mind* is the album that allowed Prince to cross over as a rock 'n' roll star, "When You Were Mine" is the song that allowed Prince to cross over as a rock 'n' roll songwriter. At San Francisco club the Stone in March 1981, Greil Marcus reported, "'That was the history of rock 'n' roll in one song!' a friend shouted before the last notes of 'When You Were Mine' were out of the air." (It should be noted that Greil, not his friend, wrote *The History of Rock 'n' Roll in Ten Songs*, a book that makes no mention of "When You Were Mine.") The song became an instant standard; the first cover appeared in less than a year, by English power-poppers Bette Bright and the Illuminations on Korova, Echo and the Bunnymen's label. It was produced by Clive Langer and Alan Winstanley, the duo behind Dexys Midnight Runners's "Come on Eileen" and Madness's "Our House" (and later, uh, Bush's *Sixteen Stone*). Other great versions would come from Detroit garage rocker Mitch Ryder and Cyndi Lauper (both 1983) and Crooked Fingers (2002), who performed it as a creaking mountain ballad.

Bette Bright's version changes the lyric slightly: instead of "I know that you're going with another guy," it becomes "I'm going with another guy"; instead of "following him whenever he's with you," another pronoun switch. Changing the lyric of "When You Were Mine" has happened a lot when people cover the song, and not just because the song's narrator was a man. The original song wasn't merely a love triangle but an ambiguously bisexual one, the interpretation of which focuses on the line "When he was there sleeping in between the two of us," as well as the end of the final verse: "Now I spend my time following him whenever he's with you." Though "Sister" was the *Dirty Mind* track where Prince spells it out ("She's the reason for my bisexuality," often transcribed as "my, uh, sexuality"), the subtle hints in "When You Were Mine" were apparently enough to keep the song off the air. As, maybe, did the song's *laissez-faire* attitude toward cheating, which reads like a peeved footnote to *The Ethical Slut*. Positioning the song's narrator as even a little queer was another touchstone with the notably gay-friendly space of new wave. The lyrics' ambiguities are clearly deliberate.

Sleeping in between the two of us: this was Prince's philosophy in a nutshell. "When You Were Mine" set up a career of defying expectations, jostling between sacred and profane, black and white, rock and funk, good or bad—and for the rest of the eighties he'd take more chances than anybody in pop. "When I brought it to the record company it shocked a lot of people," Prince told *Rolling Stone* of *Dirty Mind*. "But they didn't ask me to go back and change anything, and I'm real grateful. Anyway, I wasn't being deliberately provocative. I was being deliberately *me*." ✐

MICHAELANGELO MATOS *is the author of* The Underground Is Massive: How Electronic Dance Music Conquered America. *He lives in Brooklyn.*

How Else Will You Sense the Danger?

To Los Crudos/Limp Wrist frontman Martin Sorrondeguy, punk is obstacle and salve, audience and subject—a site of concentrated ignorance and photogenic fraternity.

BY SAM LEFEBVRE

ILLUSTRATIONS BY CAMILLA PERKINS

Martin Sorrondeguy grew up in Chicago's Pilsen neighborhood, where his family arrived after fleeing their native Uruguay. Around 1991, he started Los Crudos, a trenchant hardcore band that savaged machinations of the state, treated underserved communities with unflagging empathy, and lampooned conservative attitudes within the punk scene.

They toured five continents and established Lengua Armada Discos, a record label that Sorrondeguy still runs. Sorrondeguy chronicled it all himself in video, film, and ink. He is a documentarian by default, and his San Francisco apartment is an artifact of his enthusiasm: every surface teems with pictures and ephemera that project the sound and motion of punk.

Sorrondeguy's photography began as a practical reckoning with the reality of whose stories get told and whose do not. Today, it's a crucial, expanding body of work. Crudos disbanded in 1998—wary of what Sorrondeguy called "the rock 'n' roll format" undermining the band's capacity for activism—but Sorrondeguy remained a fixture in punk, not least as the vocalist in iconic queer hardcore act Limp Wrist. He's a historian steeped under pressure, hard-boiled by the looming threat of erasure.

Through with his ongoing participation in the punk scene, Sorrondeguy gained a nuanced, intersectional view of a subculture that's too often reduced to a few simple narratives. His sensitivity is evident in *Beyond the Screams* (1999), the documentary he made about Latino punks' resistance to American immigration policy and prejudice, and through the still images anthologized in *Get Shot* (2013), a book of photography released by Make-a-Mess Records. It would be easy to call Sorrondeguy the voice of Latino punk, but really he's its amplifier—his work calls

attention to a historically marginalized narrative in which Los Crudos played a pivotal role.

In June, Sorrondeguy and Toronto-based musician/photographer Don Pyle presented a slideshow of their respective photography at San Francisco's Center for Sex and Culture. The event homed in on the fraternal underpinning of live punk and hardcore and how the artists' own queerness situated them in scenes that were alternately hospitable and hostile to queer people of color. Sorrondeguy emphasized the need for queer activism: "It's still so stigmatized, in society at large and especially in Latino communities, even the left parts or among punks. ... As much as some punks want to say they're anarchists or whatever—you can circle the 'A' as much as you want but that fucking cross is still on your back."

Sorrondeguy has mined his collection of punk artifacts for Los Crudos' new release, *Doble LP Discografía*—a complete discography of Crudos recordings that also includes updated lyric translations and reproduces dozens of show flyers in the booklet. The album is being released by (and as a benefit for) punk's unofficial paper of record, *Maximum Rocknroll*.

[Ed. note: this article contains material from two separate conversations between the author and Martin Sorrendeguy.]

The early 1990s is often remembered as a time when political correctness swept in, especially in punk. How do you remember that era?

You have to look at the context. What was left at the end of the mid-to-late-eighties punk scene was a fucking disaster. All of the old-schoolers left, and what they left behind were the dregs, the most violent people—it was the height of American skinhead culture, if you want to call it a culture. I would never have come out of the closet at that time. Back then, you'd witness people getting beat up at shows.

When that era passed we could finally exhale. There was finally space and time for a lot of communities—like feminists in punk, queers in punk, Latinos in punk—that didn't exist prior. We could talk about things openly and not worry about getting beat up. We talked about immigration issues, that was very real to us. That was when Pete Wilson was governor of California and anti-immigrant propositions like 187 were happening right then and there.

That really was a time when we had no problem with saying, "Los Crudos is defining punk for Los Crudos and its community." We were faced with people talking shit, who just wanted to hear our band without the message, and we told them it wasn't their show. It needed to happen.

Punk, historically, is all about the individual—you singing these songs about communities, families, the perspectives of mothers is a striking contrast to that.

Immigration and deportation are bigger issues that don't have to do with punk. They don't give a fuck if you're an individual. I'm not going to speak for every Latino person, but these issues were things that our parents faced, our aunts and uncles faced, we faced, or a distant cousin faced. A lot of our audience were kids who came from communities like ours, in Texas, New Mexico, Arizona, Los Angeles, New York. We didn't have the luxury to pick and choose our politics—we had to deal with what was in our face and in our homes.

Crudos toured so extensively, it did a lot to raise and establish visibility for Latino punk—you were the ambassadors.

In the States, anywhere outside of Chicago we were play-ing shows to forty or fifty people. When we went to Mexico City, we played for one thousand fucking crazy-ass Mexican punk kids! That had to do with bootlegging. Our first demo tape and our first seven-inch went from Chicago out into the world, and kids in Mexico started dubbing it and dubbing it. Next thing you know there's a thirtieth-generation copy that sounds like fucking garbage and some kid is rocking it on a boombox. Playing Chile or Peru, people knew every single word. They got it. Kids in South Central LA or East LA or the South Side of Chicago did too. They're going, *This is the fucking real shit right here.* Not to discredit amazing supporters throughout the US and in Japan or wherever, but it had a different weight.

Yet in the reissue liner notes Golnar Nikpour had to address this myth that you guys "invented" Latino punk.

Latino punk existed in Latin America almost as soon as punk was a thing. Chicano and Latino punks have been there since the beginning in Los Angeles, but the lyrical content wasn't always focused on those communities' experiences. The Brat did a great song called "The Wolf and the Lamb"—it's in English, but it's talking about immigration. The Plugz did "La Bamba" with altered lyrics in the seventies. There was Huasipungo starting in the nineties. Dogma Mundista in LA did half-and-half songs in Spanish and English. If you put all of those pieces together you can create a lineage.

What inspired you to document that lineage with *Beyond the Screams*?

I needed to do it because people were going to forget. I'd seen a period when people didn't care about punk anymore. All of the old punks had gone and young kids were only into what was happening right then—it seemed like the *now* was so important that no one was looking back. A few of us were constantly looking back. There was a generation of kids who didn't care. I didn't want to see that happen again.

Looking back at hardcore in the eighties, it actually seems regressive in a way, like it was a more conservative movement than some punk scenes in the late seventies.

I love hardcore but it's very complicated. Think about the times: if you were even slightly odd in the eighties, people would beat you up and harass you. I was a punk. I was a target and I was going to get fucked with. If you're young and easily impressionable and not a strong person, that can make you act like an asshole at the show. If you're already angry with mainstream society and you get picked on for looking like a freak, you take that to the show and look for something to do with that aggression. Later on, as it shifted, people started reclaiming that attitude in punk and hardcore and making it their own.

So you're saying that while the aggression fostered negative attitudes, it also collected energy that could be put to better use?

It regeared the energy. Early on in the nineties, we actually just bored the really violent fuckheads. They didn't want to go to our shows. We talked to them to death. They said they didn't want to hear the talking and we went, "Bye. This isn't for you anymore." They left and it was okay for a lot of people.

When you realized the punk scene wasn't what you expected, did you consciously decide to reform it?

I thought punk was a place you could go to that would be about radicalism—radical looks, radical ideas, radical sounds, radical *everything*. When I got into it, the aesthetics were radical but I started hearing people say things that had nothing to do with radical ideas. People were following a stale pattern, one that really related to traditional American ideas. I was into peace-punk, like Crass, Conflict, the Instigators, Icons of Filth. I thought the scene in Chicago would be like that. *Wrong*. But I wanted that, so I just took it there.

Those anarcho-punk bands had topical songs, but they also put a lot of effort into parsing politics in the abstract. With Crudos, you don't get that. It's more urgent.

When Crudos started we had a song called "Don't Come and Save Us," and it's basically saying, "We, a conscious community, need new ways to deal with the problems of right now." Right then I didn't care about Marx and Lenin. We weren't about anarchism. There were people who wanted us to be part of the Communist Youth Brigade. We didn't want to align with any sort of political group. We needed

new chants, to figure out how to save ourselves, and we didn't need solutions from these old communist people.

The Crudos flyers reproduced in the liner notes of *Doble LP Discografía* are mostly benefits for things like women's shelters or indigenous peoples' organizations. Was that a guiding principle for Crudos?

If it wasn't a benefit, and it was a local show, the majority of the money was given to touring bands. That's just the way we were.

Since reuniting, you've mostly played benefits, too—I understand that the compilation benefits *Maximum Rocknroll*?

The agreement between members of Los Crudos was that if we were going to bring the band back together it had to be done in Crudos style. That was the condition. We could've done it ourselves but we wanted to do it with *MRR* and help them out a bit, which continues in the Crudos tradition of giving a lot of our shit away.

With the flyers that were included in the liner notes, were you trying to emphasize anything about the band in particular?

I wanted to show the diversity of the shows we played. I didn't want people to think we were all about Latino power, because we weren't only about that. There are kids who come up and think we don't want to interact with other cultures, but it wasn't the case. We weren't into separatism. At times we had to correct people on shit like that. The flyers show variety—there's Justice for Janitors.

What benefits were most meaningful to you?

The *Yo Hablo* compilation was one. We put that together. It benefited an organization that's unfortunately not there anymore, but it was a Latino women's-action group that helped people who were being abused by providing counseling, support, and safety. Six months after the record came out they invited me to a function and they gave me and Los Crudos a little gift and thanked us publicly. I was taken aback. Another time, we did a split record with Manumission and we were able to send $1,000 to the Western Shoshone Defense Project. I remember go-

BROOKLYN, NY , 2015
PHOTO BY CHRISTY THORNTON

"We didn't have the luxury to pick and choose our politics—we had to deal with what was in our face and in our homes."

ing home one day, months after I'd sent a check out, and I remember my dad saying, "Martin, some elder called you from the Shoshone." I thought he was kidding, but I called back and it was this elder who was thanking us. I remember saying I was sorry that it couldn't have been more. He said it was the most money they'd ever gotten.

That solidarity with Native American causes seems pretty unique for the era.

It was a real battle for them. One time we were on tour and we drove through the land and met the Dann sisters, Native American activists taking part in the struggle. Out in the middle of the desert there was a guy who was just staying out there to make sure their land wasn't getting taken away. This punk guy from the city had been living there for months because of our seven-inch. He was living

in a sort of underground dwelling burrowed into a hill and this guy was like, "Hey, I got your record and I read the shit in it and I came out here to help them."

With lyric translations changing over the years, did you ever suspect that people were projecting an agenda, or trying to tear down the group that way?

I think I was really lazy with translations in the past, or I'd have somebody else do it. This time I was able to do it on my own and really capture the closest I could to the meaning. Other people have done it themselves and honestly things shifted via typos when we were younger, like when one lost word changes the meaning. I did find some stuff online that was totally inaccurate, and yeah, some people seriously took it upon themselves to make certain changes, which is pretty odd. People have commented about the lyr-

ics having grammatical errors or being unsophisticated or whatever. None of us spoke perfectly grammatical Spanish. If you're coming from an academic background you might think our lyrics make us look like idiots, but we were a group of people coming from a generation that had been told we couldn't speak our own language in schools!

At your photo presentation the other night, Don Pyle said that he developed an "observational eye," which dovetailed into photography, partly because he was young, gay, and concerned about safety. Did you relate to that?

I did. If I look at different eras of punk that I've lived through, in the beginning I was aware of its very aggressive nature. To a certain extent it nurtured punkness or weirdness, but on the other hand, it almost seemed like if you were *too* weird you actually didn't fit in. I had this conversation in the early nineties with a friend before I came out, where I was like, "If I was gay I don't think I'd come out." There was no way. I was afraid for kids who seemed really effeminate. It actually seemed more open to girls who were masculine and tough, but I feared for guys who were more effeminate.

Yet you were still attracted to the aggression.

Well, yes—once I found it and tapped into it. There was a period of time when I couldn't find it, when I would go to these shows and think, *This doesn't feel crazy enough.* Then I came upon a series of shows where I realized, *This is hardcore*, and I fell into it.

When did that happen?

That would be my first Naked Raygun show. Naked Raygun shows were raining bodies. They're not the most aggressive-sounding band, but they were Chicago's band. And people lost it.

The other night during your talk, you examined the latent homosexual content in a lot of these photos you've taken. Was that something that you intuited at these early punk shows?

I wasn't very sexual in the beginning. That was not yet turned on in me. A nipple wasn't enough to take me there. In the late eighties I saw Beautiful Bert perform and he was this very large guy who was completely naked on-stage and trying to put a mic in his ass. It wasn't that it turned me on, but as I became more attuned to my sexuality I started looking for certain aesthetic things that were also sexual. I just thought of it as wanting to stare at certain people because they looked amazing.

Like Lux Interior from the Cramps in *Urgh! A Music War*.

That was frightening for me. I was in seventh or eighth grade and Lux was onstage with the leather pants hanging off of his ass. You know, I say I wasn't tuned in to stuff, and I wasn't very sexual, but actually as a kid there were certainly things that turned me on. That Lux footage, there was something very sexual about it and there was something very frightening about it, the way he jammed a mic into his mouth and breathed heavily into it. I remember seeing that and thinking, *This is strange*.

Tell me about coming out toward the end of Los Crudos. Was there backlash?

In the mid-to-late eighties, I was a teenager. I hadn't solidified strong belief systems. I had ideas but I wasn't ready to take on something like my sexuality. Later on, I was. I felt secure. I didn't care if someone stopped liking my band.

Before that revelation, you were a dancer, which is a very sensual and performative thing. I'm interested in how you left b-boy culture behind as much as how you dove into punk, and how the two connected.

There was athleticism. It was very competitive. We always had to be ready to battle. I practiced every day for hours. So it felt almost more like a sport at times, but it was nose-diving, too. People were getting tired of seeing it at clubs, so the b-boys were starting to move on and do other things. The media was promoting it nonstop, putting it in every commercial imaginable, and then suddenly it was considered lame and shitty. I sensed the shift and said at some point I knew I wanted to continue on the path I was heading, which was getting more interested in punk. Someone asked me what I was going to do next and I said, "Punk. I'm going punk." They thought it was funny. Some of those people saw me years later and realized I wasn't kidding.

You're still very much involved. There's an element of secrecy to punk and hardcore that's valuable in

"Queer punk kids need to grow a thick skin because if you are truly a weirdo, you need to learn to defend yourself."

BUENOS AIRES, 2013

PHOTO BY MARIANA MANUELA BELLONE

a lot of ways. As a documentarian, how do you juggle wanting to keep the secret and wanting to let people know it's important?

Someone once noticed that I photograph the opening bands, these bands that nobody cares about, these fucking nobody bands. I'm interested in that real initial visceral energy of a new band, the first time playing, the excitement or lack of. I'm not in search of the next big thing, that's not what I do with punk. I'm interested in new things evolving and photographing it. It's like how *Maximum Rocknroll* puts unknown bands on the cover and maybe they don't even get remembered—bands with a moment and nothing more—and that's great.

The other night, your photo presentation reminded me of what the Toronto zine *JDs* did, as far as decontextualizing these images of punks to bring out the implicit gay qualities.

There are moments that occur and they're captured and it looks really odd and it's not exactly what you think it is. There are really gay moments and I happen to catch them. It's fun to look at that and it's what we've always talked about: when things get that tough and macho they become really fraternal really fast.

You said that now straight punks even "gay it up" for your camera.

I'm lucky! I can be in completely hardcore punk spaces and kids are cool. There's a mutual respect.

It's progressive, in a juvenile sort of way. Is it ever tokenizing?

No. It's these kids letting me know it's cool. There doesn't have to be any weirdness. Also some kids want to show that they're queer too. There are some kids who aren't into it, too, but I'm not disappearing.

Right. You photographed a band in Australia that said homophobic things as they opened for Limp Wrist and they later apologized.

Yeah. In that case, we were like, "Don't apologize." We weren't interested in hearing the apology. It's not the way they really are. But what I was thinking and the reason I photographed them was like, please look at the way you are dressed right now! The singer could've walked right through Folsom and Dore Alley! The audience was more upset than we were, actually.

It's interesting that you rejected the apology, finding it disingenuous. Do you ever worry about what people call the chilling effect of political correctness? This sense that people are chastened into silence?

Yeah, there is a negative side. If people are being so cautious about what they say, then what is authentic about them? What do they really think? When you force everybody to participate in an ideology, what's the indivisible belief underneath it?

What about in the punk scene itself?

If we just want to be surrounded by back-patting punks who agree with us, then what's the point? There's no discourse. I'd rather have a punk kid say to me, "I grew up with parents who taught me how *your people* are." I want to have that conversation with that kid. If you're not questioning the utmost politically correct punks, there's a problem. Someone should question me. That's what it's about.

Safe spaces are a touchy subject for a lot of people. The first time I was shown a separate room away from the gig space where I can hang out because I'm a queer person of color, I thought, *This is fucking ridiculous.* That is offensive. Queer punk kids need to grow a thick skin because if you are truly a weirdo you need to learn to defend yourself.

That's interesting. I'm definitely not in a position to tell someone that, but do you feel compelled to say that, as someone who's been around?

It's important for me to say it, yeah. We create bubbles, but they pop easily and you need to be ready. The real world is gnarly towards queer people, so be prepared when some dude comes to beat your ass for being a sissy. I wouldn't tell young queer kids to only hang out with other young queer kids. How else are you going to sense the danger? ✍

SAM LEFEBVRE *is a freelance writer and vocational guttersnipe based in Oakland.*

Alex Chilton, Grand Central Station, 1987.
PHOTO BY GODLIS